WRITING REPORTS FOR COURT

An International Guide for Psychologists Who Work in the Criminal Jurisdiction

Jack White, Andrew Day, Louisa Hackett and J. Thomas Dalby

Originally published in 2007 by Australian Academic Press Pty. Ltd. as:
"Writing Reports For Courts: A Practical Guide
for Psychologists Working in Forensic Contexts".

This edition published 2015 by:
Australian Academic Press Group Pty. Ltd.
18 Victor Russell Drive
Samford Valley QLD 4520, Australia
www.australianacademicpress.com.au

Copyright © 2015 Jack White, Andrew Day, Louisa Hackett, and J. Thomas Dalby

Copying for educational purposes
The *Australian Copyright Act 1968* (Cwlth) allows a maximum of one chapter or 10% of this book, whichever is the greater, to be reproduced and/or communicated by any educational institution for its educational purposes provided that the educational institution (or the body that administers it) has given a remuneration notice to Copyright Agency Limited (CAL) under the Act.
For details of the CAL licence for educational institutions contact:
Copyright Agency Limited, 19/157 Liverpool Street, Sydney, NSW 2000.
E-mail info@copyright.com.au

Production and communication for other purposes
Except as permitted under the Act, for example a fair dealing for the purposes of study, research, criticism or review, no part of this book may be reproduced, stored in a retrieval system, or transmitted in any form or by any means electronic, mechanical, photocopying, recording or otherwise without prior written permission of the copyright holder.

Writing Reports for Court: An International Guide for Psychologists Who Work in the Criminal Jurisdiction

ISBN   9781922117403 (paperback)
ISBN   9781922117410 (ebook)

Dewey Number   614.1

Publisher: Stephen May

Copy Editor: Rhonda McPherson

Graphic Designer: Maria Biaggini, The Letter Tree

Typesetting: Australian Academic Press

Printing: Lightning Source

Cover image: © Jack White

Foreword

For three of the four authors of this book it is their second book on the topic. In 2007 Jack White, Andrew Day and Louisa Hackett published *Writing Reports for Court: A Practical Guide For Psychologists Working in Forensic Contexts*. In this more recent book, they are joined by J. Thomas Dalby from Canada. Hence the 'Practical' guide becomes the 'International' guide. That is not simply because a Canadian perspective has been included with the assistance of J. Thomas Dalby. This guide includes detailed descriptions of relevant law and practice in the United States, the United Kingdom, New Zealand and Singapore. Despite the substitution of 'International' for 'Practical' this addition contains all the helpful material of its predecessor. Material has been expanded and updated. Both books wisely include sections on psychologists giving evidence, pointing out how essential to effective court presentation is a well prepared report. Those psychologists who have given evidence in contested hearings, well know how the strengths and weaknesses of their reports have enhanced or weakened their evidence. Skilled cross-examiners do not spend much time on the well reasoned, well authenticated passages in a report. They focus on the gaps in history taking or the insufficiently supported conclusions. This book is a very helpful guide to psychologists in avoiding those and other pitfalls.

The other difference in the subtitle of this book reflects a focus this time on the criminal jurisdiction. Whereas the predecessor volume dealt with the civil and matrimonial jurisdictions those topics are omitted here. I think there is sense in that. The general advice given to psychologists working in the criminal jurisdiction will remain helpful for those working in the civil and matrimonial jurisdictions, but the practice and protocols of those jurisdictions are sufficiently different to require detailed and separate treatment.

Judges and magistrates sometimes criticise psychologists' reports for being too long. Those criticisms may turn out to be well founded if the area of dispute in court is reduced or if the charges faced by the defendant are quite minor. Occasionally a psychological report is commissioned when more extensive submissions by counsel would suffice. However the psychologist is in a difficult position. He or she cannot be quite sure how detailed his or her report should be. It should also be borne in mind that psychological reports are not only read by those associated with the court process. The reports are forwarded to Community Corrections if the defendant is placed on a supervised bond. The reports go to the prison authorities and the Parole Board if the defendant is imprisoned. The reports are then needed by the professional people charged with supervising or housing the defendant. Individual parts of a report may be of limited assistance to the court but they are of greater value to others down the track.

The authors of this book have, I think, got the balance right. They have provided guidance for the preparation of thorough, professional reports. It is up to the experienced psychologist to compose the report best suited to the needs of the client and the occasion that brings him or her before the court. This book, like its predecessor, will help practitioners in that task. The authors are to be congratulated on the wealth of experience they have passed on. Psychological reports, and psychologists' evidence, will be enhanced by this work.

Judge Gordon Barrett
Judge of the District Court of South Australia

Contents

Foreword iv

Preface vii

About the Authors viii

Chapter 1   Introduction   1

Difference Between a Witness of Fact and an Expert Witness 2
Guidelines for Expert Witnesses 4
The Report Structure 5
The Introduction 6
Background Material 9
Current Legal Matter 15

Chapter 2   The Psychological Assessment   17

Behaviour During the Assessment 17
Essential Elements of Psychological Tests 18
Performance Based Tests 23
Availability of Treatment or Rehabilitation 31
Impression Management and Malingering 32
Psycho-Legal Tests 34

Chapter 3   Opinion   37

Court Report: Mr Jack Jones 37
Court Report: Mr William Pitt 50
Court Report: Mr Leonard Panther 60
Court Report: Mr Jason Collins 73
Court Report: Mr Arthur Askey 83

Chapter 4   Going to Court as an Expert Witness   97

Know the Legal Landscape 98
Pre-Trial Consultation 99
Preparation 99
Getting Qualified or 'Proofed' as an Expert 100
The Scientific Expert 102
Examination in Chief 103
Cross-Examination 104
Re-Direct 107
Post-Trial Consultation 107
Advanced Performance 108

Chapter 5   Report Writing in Different Jurisdictions   111

United States of America..111
Canada..119
United Kingdom 127
Australia 131
New Zealand...134
Singapore..139

References   147

Appendix — Example Practice Direction   153

Glossary of Psychological Tests   157

Index   163

Preface

Psychologists are increasingly being asked to give evidence in court. For some this is an exciting and rewarding activity, both personally and professionally, and yet for many others it can be a harrowing experience. This books outlines some of the most important things to consider when preparing a court report and giving evidence. It provides guidance on the content and structure of reports, highlighting the importance of assessments that directly address the legal questions that are under consideration. Appearing in court is much more rewarding for those who are well prepared and when the evidence they present is clearly linked to the reasons they have been called! We hope you find this book useful.

About the Authors

Jack White is the principal of White & Associates Psychologists, a specialist forensic psychology practice based in Adelaide. He has a Doctorate Degree in Psychology from the University of Adelaide and is a Fellow of the Australian Psychological Society. He received the 2008 Award of Distinction from the Australian Psychological Society's College of Forensic Psychologists and is a past National Chair of that College. He taught within the Forensic Psychology Masters program (1999–2010) at the University of South Australia, and currently is an Adjunct Associate Professor of Clinical Psychology at the University of Canberra. Academically he has published widely in areas that include report writing, psychometric assessment, Indigenous neuropsychology, mental impairment, intellectual disability, and criminal behavior in athletes.

Andrew Day is Professor in the School of Psychology at Deakin University and a Fellow of the Australian Psychological Society. He has published widely in the area of offender rehabilitation. Before joining academia he was employed as a clinical psychologist in South Australia and the UK, having gained his Doctorate in Clinical Psychology from the University of Birmingham and a Masters in Applied Criminological Psychology from the University of London.

Louisa Hackett is the Principal Psychologist for Youth Justice in South Australia. While gaining her Masters in Forensic Psychology, she worked as a Research Associate in the Forensic Psychology Research Group at the University of South Australia. Since then, she has worked primarily in correctional and forensic mental health settings, conducting psychological assessments and providing intervention with adults and young people involved in the criminal justice system for the last 10 years.

J. Thomas Dalby has provided expert opinions to courts across Canada and the United States for 36 years relating to criminal, civil and administrative law matters. Dr Dalby is an Adjunct Professor of Psychology at the University of Calgary and was on the faculty of Medicine for 26 years. He has published over 100 books, chapters, and articles in medical, legal and psychological forums. In 2013 Dr Dalby received the highest Canadian award for a professional psychologist — the Canadian Psychological Association's award for distinguished contributions to psychology. He has also published fiction and was co-writer of an award-winning screenplay based on a key insanity case in London in 1843.

Chapter 1

Introduction

This book has been written to help psychologists to present the results of their assessments as evidence in court. The report is the most important way in which he or she can communicate the outcomes of a psychological assessment. It is the report that is submitted as evidence, and a poor quality report can have negative implications not only for the individual psychologist but for the profession as a whole. Although the chapters that follow identify a range of issues that are relevant to report writing across a number of different countries, it is immediately apparent that high quality reports have many things in common. A good report will, for example, clearly examine psychological issues that are of direct relevance to the legal decision-making, taking account of the germane local legislation. Indeed, it is legislation that provides definition and direction for the report. The psychologist brings together in a good report general factual and clinical material and considers its relevance to the legal issues under consideration, with the aim of providing a coherent and logical opinion for the court.

Good reports follow a logical structure which clearly documents the reasons for the referral, the nature of the assessment, and the opinion of the expert. The chapters that follow describe an approach that provides such a structure, as well as guidance on how to use a range of psychological tools/methods that can inform an opinion. While psychological reports can be prepared to address a wide range of legal questions that arise in different courts and tribunals, our focus here is solely on those reports that are prepared for the criminal court.

What makes forensic reports different from general clinical reports has mostly to do with their content and style. The content is often dissimilar from that contained in general psychological reports because of the overriding need to address forensic questions. The style differs because forensic reports are written to meet the demands of legal forums, non-expert readers and decision-makers. Unlike reports that seek to communicate with like-minded professionals, the court report is written for the lay person and should, therefore, be written in a manner that is readily understandable and free from jargon. The use of legal terminology, with moderation, willhowever increase the credibility of the report. A series of case examples are used in this book to illustrate these differences.

Finally, this book considers how to effectively give oral evidence in court based on the report and how the psychologist might prepare him or herself to do this professionally. We begin, however, by discussing the different roles that the psychologist can play in the legal process.

Difference Between a Witness of Fact and an Expert Witness

In normal court proceedings witnesses are not permitted to offer opinions; rather they can only provide evidence about factual matters. A psychologist may be called to give evidence in a court as a *witness of fact* rather than as an expert and, as such, must limit his or her evidence to what has been observed. For example, the psychologist may be required to give evidence as to when and how often he or she met the defendant and provide details of the treatment provided. The psychologist should not, however, offer an opinion to the court about the legal issues under consideration unless he or she is also qualified as an expert. For some psychologists this distinction seems unfair, but it is intended to ensure that experts work within their field of expertise and are aware of the legal matters being addressed.

An *expert witness* is a witness who is recognised by the court as a person who can give an opinion in a specific area of knowledge that the court determines lies outside the understanding of the common man. Across the Western world, courts have determined that psychology is a scientific discipline about which the common man may not have adequate understanding. The psychologist can thus act as an expert witness if the court acknowledges that he or she has the relevant qualifications, training, and experience. Courts must, however, determine the psychologist's expert status each time he or she appears. It is not unusual for this to be contested — especially in situations in which the psychologist has limited experience. It will then be responsibility of the judge to decide whether or not the psychologist is accepted as an expert.

In order to establish expertise, the lawyer offering the psychologist as an expert will usually present the court with the curriculum vitae. This should contain details about academic qualifications, registration, professional affiliations, employment background, academic appointments, clinical appointments, past experience as an expert in the court and a listing of publications, scientific papers, presentations and workshops, as well as information about relevant experience in acting as an expert witness.

It is generally recommended that those involved with the care and treatment of an individual should not undertake a psychological assessment for court; Greenberg and Shuman (1997) have presented a powerful case that the roles of the 'assessor' and the 'treating practitioner' are so different that they should not be combined (see Table 1.1). That is to say that treating practitioners should refrain from offering legal opinion (i.e., restricting themselves to acting solely as witnesses of fact in legal settings), and that practitioners who undertake evaluative roles for the courts, should not sub-

	Care Provision	Forensic Evaluation
1. Whose client is the patient/litigant?	The mental health practitioner	The attorney
2. The relational privilege that governs disclosure in each relationship	Therapist-patient privilege	Attorney–client and attorney work–product privilege
3. The cognitive set and evaluative attitude of each expert	Supportive, accepting, empathic	Neutral, objective, detached
4. The differing areas of competency of each expert	Therapy techniques for treatment of the impairment	Forensic evaluation techniques relevant to the legal claim
5. The nature of hypotheses tested by each expert	Diagnostic criteria for the purpose of therapy	Psycho-legal criteria for purpose of legal adjudication
6. The scrutiny applied to the information utilized in the process and the role of historical truth	Mostly based on information from the person being treated with little scrutiny of that information by the therapist	Litigant information supplemented with that of collateral sources and scrutinised by the evaluator and the court
7. The amount and control of structure in each relationship	Therapist attempts to benefit the patient by working within the therapeutic relationship	Evaluator advocates for the results and implications of the evaluation for the benefit of the court
8. The nature and degree of 'adversarialness' in each relationship	A helping relationship; rarely adversarial	An evaluative relationship; frequently adversarial
9. The goal of the professional in each relationship	Therapist attempts to benefit the patient by working within the therapeutic relationship	Evaluator advocates for the results and implications of the evaluator for the benefits of the court
10. The impact on each relationship of critical judgment by the expert	The basis of the relationship is the therapeutic alliance and critical judgment is likely to impair that alliance	The basis of the relationship is evaluative and critical judgment is unlikely to cause serious emotional harm

Note: Adapted from Greenberg & Shuman, 1997. The general term attorney is used in the U.S. and some other jurisdictions to refer to a lawyer.

Table 1.1 Differences between Therapeutic and Forensic Relationships

sequently make themselves available for therapeutic work. The psychologist can, of course, carry out these distinct roles with separate individuals (i.e., provide treatment to some individuals and evaluate others).

Our own experience of working in clinical and forensic settings has shown that rarely are these roles adequately separated, leading to a wide variability in the quality and utility of reports submitted to the courts. At the very least though there is a need for all parties to be clear about the nature and extent of dual or multiple roles. We believe that considering the impact of dual relationships can help to clarify the nature of any real or potential conflicts of interest and help to allay any criticisms of partisanship that may undermine professionalism. Of course, in practice, things are not always clear-cut. Sometimes clients are involved in litigation when they enter therapy. At other times they may become involved in legal proceedings shortly afterwards. It is important that such clients are aware that the confidentiality of their sessions may be compromised if their mental health is raised as an issue relevant to any litigation. Psychologists should try to identify these clients early by asking at the beginning of treatment if clients are, or are likely to become, involved in legal proceedings.

As we have already noted, an expert report differs from a clinical report in so far as the main issues addressed are those which are directly relevant to the legal case. Whereas in mental health settings the client is primarily the individual being assessed, in forensic work the 'client' is often considered to be the court. Accordingly, the court report is not a confidential document and the client should *always* be informed that anything she or he tells the psychologist might be included. In fact, in most jurisdictions there is a requirement that the expert witness reveals everything that has been recorded if asked in testimony — even if it was not used in final report. Typically psychologists give opinions only on people they have evaluated personally, but they may, under some circumstances, conduct a file review, or otherwise give an opinion on scientific issues relevant to the case at bar (see Dalby & Nesca, 2008).

Guidelines for Expert Witnesses

Before describing how to conduct an assessment and prepare a court report, it is important to be aware of any report writing guidelines. We strongly suggest that anyone who intends acting as an expert witness becomes familiar with those that apply to the jurisdiction in which they practice. The *practice direction* helps to ensure that *data* is used as the basis of the opinion, rather than personal beliefs or values that cannot be substantiated. Practice directions typically require the expert to state his or her academic and professional qualifications, professional affiliations and other relevant supplementary information that can help to establish his or her credibility (see the Appendix for an example practice direction). In some jurisdictions it is a requirement that the author acknowledges that he or she has read the relevant practice direction or that he or she is aware that their duty is to the court. This shows that the expert understands that the role is neutral and agrees to follow the court guidelines. It also helps to ensure that experts are (perceived to be) fair and honest in their work, and not biased in favour of the party that engaged them. It is nonetheless important to appreciate that different parties will ask questions which suit the interests of those they represent; while the expert may answer in a way that may appear to support a particular case, the data itself should never be distorted. It is quite possible that the court will ask that data be re-examined by another expert who is then asked to comment on the appropriateness of the opinion formed.

The Report Structure

Grisso (2010) has argued that there is now a general 'consensus' amongst forensic psychologists about how an expert witness report should be organised. The report should, for example, include an 'Introduction', a section reporting 'Data', and another providing the 'Opinion'. The Introduction should identify the reason for the referral, the sources of data used to inform the opinion, and the manner in which the examinee was informed of the limits of confidentiality. The Data section should describe all relevant data that were obtained to address the forensic question. Finally, the Opinion section should provide the psychologist's interpretation of what is relevant to the referral question.

This general structure is not fixed, but should be adapted to local jurisdictional demands, different types of referral question, and the psychologist's own preferences for the sequencing of content that best communicates his or her assessment of a particular case. Indeed, Grisso (2010) notes that there is nothing particularly 'forensic' about this way of organising forensic reports. It is similar in structure to the clinical report, and bears some resemblance to how psychological research is presented in academic journals. As noted above, what makes forensic reports different, however, is their content and style:

> The content is often different because of the need to address forensic questions that require different data than most clinical reports. The style differs because forensic reports are written to meet the demands of legal forums, non-clinical readers and decision makers, and due-process constraints (Grisso, 2010, pp.103–104).

While this may sound obvious, there is good reason to believe that many psychological reports do not meet these basic criteria. Grisso (2010) reports that "poor organisation of material" in forensic reports is a common problem — more than a third of reports that did not meet the 'pass' criteria determined by a select group of examiners from the American Board of Forensic Psychology were poorly organised. Over half of the reports that did not pass the review did not clearly state the referral question. Thus, in this book we argue that just as scientific research reports for journal articles adhere to a well-defined structure, so too should the psychological report for court.

Consistent with Grisso's suggestions, we suggest that the essential components of a court report are:

1. *Introduction*, which comprises the following sub-sections:
   (a) referral details
   (b) the information sources
   (c) a statement recognising any legal acknowledgements in relation to the expert having read any specific practice directions recommended by the court
   (d) a statement of the expert's qualifications and relevant experience
   (e) a statement around issues of confidentiality and patients signed acknowledgment
2. *Data*, which used to inform the assessment, including:
   (a) client history
   (b) psychological test results
   (c) third party information or collateral information
3. *Opinion*, which presents:
   (a) a summary of relevant data
   (b) a discussion about relevant opinion options
   (c) an expert opinion on relevant psycho-legal issues

We will now discuss each of these sections in greater detail.

The Introduction
Referral Details
The court report should begin by unambiguously advising the reader of the purpose of the report — why it was requested and by whom. The report should therefore state the name of the person or organisation requesting the report and details of the particular issues that the psychologist will provide an opinion about. It should then clearly state the specific questions that the psychologist was asked to address. Relevant regulations, case law, or statutes within the jurisdiction will often define these questions, depending on where the assessment was conducted. The forensic questions should always guide the report. The report should then go on to provide information about the examinee's identity.

Information Sources
This section of the report should list comprehensively all the resources and references that were used in the assessment. This can be inserted at the beginning of the report or as an appendix at the end. These may include:

- correspondence (cited and dated)
- health reports (e.g., medical / mental health / education, with authors names and dates)
- details associated with the interviews (dates)
- details about the psychological tests used (version of tests, publication dates, etc.).
- tests administration details (dates, details of test assessors)
- other third party reports (e.g., police reports, witness statements, all accurately dated).
- research articles relevant to legal questions or issues (full references & dates)
- identification of the patient (e.g., driver's licence)

There should be no information omitted from this section, even if it appears unimportant.

Awareness of Practice Direction

In most jurisdictions the court will provide guidelines for expert witnesses to follow. These set out specific methodology and rules that the expert must follow in order to satisfy the court that he or she is fulfilling the role of an expert witness. For example, it may be essential for the expert to give particulars of any identifying material upon which the expert based his or her expert opinion, to indicate whether there were any tests or experiments that the expert relied upon in compiling the report, and to provide details in the report of the qualifications of the person who carried out any such tests or experiment. Direction may also given to an expert in relation to defining his or her specific duty to the court, such as in the statement below. You may simply state that you are aware of this directive and have conducted your assessment accordingly.

> An expert witness has an overriding duty to assist the court on matters relevant to the expert's areas of expertise. An expert witness is not an advocate for a party. An expert witness's paramount duty is to the court and not to the person retaining the expert.

Statement of Qualification

The introductory section of the report should include a detailed statement of the expert's qualifications. This is very important, as it outlines the reason why you should be accepted as an expert, and therefore as someone who is qualified to provide an opinion to the court. The statement should include all the relevant essential information, including:

- academic qualifications, including where and when they were obtained
- relevant professional associations that the expert belongs to and any professional/academic awards
- current employment and relevant past employment positions
- any research carried out by the expert relevant to the opinion being expressed
- a summary of the expert's field of expertise
- the history and frequency of providing evidence in court (within various jurisdictions).

As an example:

> "I am a registered psychologist in the Province of Ontario and have been since 1983. Additionally, I have been a Diplomate of the American Board of Professional Psychology with a specialty in Forensic Psychology since 1989. I hold the rank of Professor in the Department of Psychology at York University. I am a Fellow of the Canadian Psychological Association and the American Psychological Association. I am the author of over 100 professional books, chapters and articles in medical, psychological and legal forums. I have conducted over 10,000 forensic evaluations and provided viva voce testimony on over 700 occasions. I enclose a copy of my full Curriculum vitae and it can also be view at my university web page – htttp://psych.yorku.ca/Alexander–Pearson"

Finally, it is recommended that a more comprehensive curriculum vitae be attached as an appendix to the report (and/or referred to in your report as a web based document that is easily accessible). This may also be used when the expert's credentials are being examined in court. A full listing of relevant publications and presentations can provide added weight to the expert's opinion. Any publications specifically relevant to the case may be highlighted for the reader (e.g., 'of particular relevance to this matter, I published an article on the recidivism rates of incest offenders — see p. 10 of CV').

Issues of Confidentiality

As a writer of what may become a public document, the limits of confidentiality are different for the forensic report writer. Whereas treating psychologists have a duty to protect the interests of their client, an expert witness has an over-riding duty to the court and understands that this many mean providing evidence that harms the client's case. Thus, there are significant limitations to the confidentially of *any* information disclosed during the assessment, and psychologists who act as expert witnesses are ethically obliged to inform clients that they are required to tell the truth. Typically any evaluation should begin with the expert stating something along the lines of the following:

> I am a forensic psychologist who has been asked by [the court/your attorney] to conduct a psychological evaluation. I will be preparing a report based on the information you provide me with, together with the psychometric test results. As such anything you tell me may be disclosed in my report. That is, there is no confidentiality with information you may provide. If you do not wish to discuss any matters with me, I will respect your right not to.

In the body of the report, a statement should be made by the writer to indicate that the expert explained to the client the limitations of confidentiality prior to the commencement of the assessment, and that this information was also presented in written form. It is good practice to ask the client to sign a statement acknowledging his or her awareness of these limitations. It is important to inform clients that a report that is requested by the court will *always* be used in evidence, whereas a report prepared for the defence counsel may not necessarily be revealed. As an expert, it is relatively unusual to receive any feedback as to whether or not your report was used (unless of course you are required to give oral evidence in relation to the report), or even to hear the outcome of the case.

Background Material

An expert's analytical processing is akin to solving a complex jigsaw puzzle. The assessment process begins with determining the critical pieces of the puzzle and then putting them together in a logical manner. The pieces include information from a variety of sources: client history, psychometric testing, relevant legal criteria and collateral information. So what are the core elements or pieces of the jigsaw puzzle needed to provide an opinion about how a psychological profile may be relevant to the legal issues under consideration?

The starting point of any assessment is the personal history of the client. A detailed account of the psychological and inter-personal context in which the legal issues arose is important if any results related to the assessment are to be meaningfully interpreted. Potentially relevant information includes the *family* history (e.g., the individual's relationship with parents / siblings / grandparents). Taking a history of relationships, schooling, and employment is also important. From a psychological perspective, it is important to understand physical and mental health, childhood behavioural problems and any exposure to trauma or abuse, as well as substance use. The impact of life events is also important to assess. These might include, for example, family trauma (the death of a spouse, child, parent or friend), relationship changes (divorce, partner separation); family changes (marriage, pregnancy, birth); education (school failure, school changes, bullying); employment issues (workload excesses, conflict, dismissal, retirement); health and mental health issues (injury or illness, victim of abuse whether it be physical, sexual or emotional; exposure to trauma (e.g., flood, fire disasters, victim of crime, motor vehicle accident etc.); financial issues (e.g., loss of housing ; foreclosure on a mortgage or loan; financial debts e.g., drugs, gambling, legal costs); substance usage (excessive alcohol and drugs issues); and legal issues (e.g., court trial, incarceration). Personality traits, such as impulsivity or the tendency to get angry, are of particular interest as they can help to inform judgments of how the individual might react in different situations. Finally, the assessment should consider the offending history (especially convictions and sentences) and attendance and completion of any offending behaviour or rehabilitation programs. It is often also important to consider the client's *motivation* to not offend and the level of support that is available from family, friends, and professionals to achieve this. We will now consider each of these areas of assessment in turn.

Personal and Family History

Parental and caregiver relationships have a powerful influence on psychological development. The assessor may be interested in:

- Whether each parent is alive.
- Whether the parents are together or not, and if not, when they were separated.
- If separation occurred, what impact this had on the client.
- The client's relationship with each parent through childhood.
- The current relationship with each parent.
- When the client last had contact with each parent.
- How the client views his or her siblings.
- When the client last had contact with each sibling.

Associated with these questions will be a network of alternative and supplementary questions (e.g., in cases of separation, what was the client's relationship with any step-parents?). These may help to understand the development and maintenance of any dysfunctional or antisocial behaviour. As families are often the principal source of support for individuals during periods of stress, the assessment should try to clarify how the client perceives the support that is available.

The next set of questions should ask about significant relationships. Significant relationships may be defined as being those that have longevity, including those which have produced a child or children. The assessor might review:

- the child's age
- the child's personality and behaviour
- the child's level of functioning and school performance
- the child's relationship with the client.

For each significant relationship accurate information should be obtained. Questions may include:

- when the relationship began
- when the relationship ended and why
- how the client perceived the relationship
- how the client perceived the stability and general harmony of the relationship.

Questions such as: 'When did you last see and speak with your former partner?' may provide a simple objective indication of closeness. If, for example, the client states that his or her relationship was 'very close' but also states that he or she has 'not had any contact for the past six months' further questioning may assist in determining the relationship's actual strength.

Details about the home or place where the client resides is the final component of the family history. Such information may assist understanding the client's general level of stability and contentment with life. Details of interest here include:

- the nature of the residence (house, apartment, owned or rented)
- how long the client has lived there
- other occupants
- satisfaction with the place of residence

Education

Obtaining information about a person's educational background can be very helpful when trying to understand the individual's personal history. Detailed information related to the client's primary and secondary education should include:

- the number of schools attended and when
- the type of school attended (private / public / religious based)
- whether the client received any special education
- friends at school

- relationship with teachers
- any behavioural problems (e.g., fighting, school disengagement, or truancy)
- ability to cope with the academic work
- favourite subjects
- highest level of the academic standard
- any expulsions or suspensions
- age when left school and the reasons for leaving.

Access to collateral information usually strengthens the accuracy and credibility of any self-report. Obtaining a client's school reports, for example, may offer important information about both the client's childhood behaviour and their academic engagement. If the assessor obtains written consent to release information, schools generally are happy to provide the assessor with reports. Parents may also assist in providing this information. Nesca and Dalby (2013) provide a comprehensive account of the use of third-party information for use in conjunction with a forensic psychological interview. They point out how this improves the validity of the 'data' that is used in psychological reports.

Vocational and Employment

Obtaining a complete vocational history can, at times, be a lengthy process. To gauge the complexity a usual starting point is to get a flavour of the person's history by asking an initial general question about the person's work history, such as "have you had many jobs over the years and what has been your the main area of your work?". It may then be relevant to itemise information about each job to determine:

- the job title and specific job function
- the name of the client's employer
- when the job started and finished
- whether the position was full or part-time (number of hours per week)
- the client's level of job satisfaction and/or stress at work
- reasons for leaving the job
- current employment status and primary income source.

Again, the ability to draw on any collateral information (e.g., vocational references) will add weight to client self-report.

Physical Health

Detailing relevant factors about a person's physical health can often provide insight into the nature of the person's general level of functioning. The following are important details:

- the client's history of past accidents and past trauma
- any specific conditions relevant to offending (e.g., hepatitis associated with drug use)
- when conditions were first diagnosed/ treated
- how the client sees him or herself in terms of level of fitness and general health.

Collateral information, including medical reports and hospital discharge statements, can usually be obtained with minimal inconvenience provided the client provides you with a signed consent form. A telephone consultation with their current physician might also be warranted.

Mental Health

Questions about a person's mental health require careful wording to obtain relevant and accurate material. For example, many people perceive mental health problems to be extreme states (e.g., schizophrenia) and so some simple initial questions about day-to-day issues can be particularly useful. A useful start is to ask about the client's current mood and what he or she considers to be major stresses. It is also important to understand any major stresses that were present at the time that the relevant offence was committed.

It is important to allow the client to feel he or she can discuss the issues in a free and emotionally safe way and to proceed at his or her own pace. Past history of involvement with mental health services, psychologists, or psychiatrists should also be clarified, and any collateral reports should be sought when necessary.

Substance Use

Obtaining details associated with a client's substance use is best conducted by taking a direct, systematic, detailed history for each substance. Clients rarely have problems providing a detailed history of their substance use. They will usually provide such information even when drug use is unrelated to their current charges. It is best to deal first with substances that are most common (and legal), before asking about those that may be illicit. Substances to be reviewed should include all of the major types of drugs. When discussing substance use refer to drugs by their street name as this is likely to have most meaning for clients. However, the final report should describe the drugs by their scientific names or common proprietary names (which vary by country). The side effects of specific drugs may be forensically at issue in many cases as they may impair cognitive functioning, induce impulsivity or aggression. The most common recreational drugs include central nervous systems *stimulants* (e.g., caffeine, tobacco, amphetamines, methamphetamines, methylphenidate ['Ritalin'], cocaine), and *depressants* (barbiturates; minor tranquillisers, such as benzodiazepines; major tranquillizers or antipsychotics; alcohol; narcotics, including opiates and opioids, methadone; hallucinogens, such as lysergic acid diethylamide (LSD); marijuana; inhalants).

Legal History

Central to an assessment is understanding the nature of the actual offending behaviour. However, it is important that the assessment considers only those offences for which the individual has been convicted and not those offences for which the individual may have been *charged* but not convicted. Past legal history should include:

- the date(s) when the individual first began offending
- the nature of specific offences for which the person has been convicted
- a statement about the consequences of the convictions (e.g., fines and periods of time spent incarcerated)
- what the client perceived were the main motivations for past offending.

In some cases, individuals may seek to minimise their past history of offending. In serious criminal matters it is particularly important that the assessor obtain a complete, accurate and up to date police record. This ensures that the history of past offending is not misrepresented. Inaccuracies in this area can only discredit the veracity of the report. Reviewing an official criminal history with an accused is particularly interesting for whether they provide full substance of the past matters or try to minimise their involvement. An item by item review beginning at their first official offence lets them know that you are aware of the full extent of the official criminal ledger.

Other Background Issues

Depending on the nature of the client's issues offence and background, additional background information may be required. This may include exploration of issues such as:

- military history
- psychological treatment
- gambling
- financial.

The psychologist should ask any questions that are likely to be of relevance. However, there is always a limit to how much information can be included in a report, and in most cases, unless there is clear relevance, general background information can be omitted.

Current Legal Matter

In criminal matters it is usually important for the assessor to obtain an accurate account of the offences for which the individual has been charged, and as well as background information related to when the alleged offending occurred. The assessor needs to know whether the client is pleading guilty or not guilty to the charges as, if this has not occurred, questioning about the alleged offending may jeopardise the client's plea. Assuming that the client is pleading guilty to the charge, the assessor should determine:

- What he or she allegedly did.
- Reasons the client provided for the offending (if it is acknowledged).
- Reactions to the charges.

The case formulation or functional assessment approach is recommended to understand why offences occurred. This method clearly and systematically identifies the pathways to offending for the individual and requires a comprehensive analysis of the antecedents of offending. It is helpful to ask the client to describe not only the offence itself, but the day leading up to the offence, and the offending period or weeks leading up to when the offence occurred.

In having an accused describe their involvement in a violent crime, we find that Meloy's (1992) model is useful. This is a simple three by three matrix with the upper lateral axis a temporal gradient (Before, During, After) and the vertical axis separating personal experiences (Thoughts, Emotions, Behaviour). In this way connections between the three types of experiences can be chained. Meloy has the client, for example, describe what the police would see as they pulled up to the scene of the violence (Behaviours) and asks then what the person thought or felt. The interplay of sequence in these responses is often very useful. The determination of whether an act of violence is reactionary or predatory can often be assisted with such methods.

Of course, retrospective reconstructions like this are influenced by a host of factors that can impact recall even in a patient who is trying their best to be accurate. The psychologist can evaluate egregious exaggerations such as the patient describing drinking 26 fl oz (770ml) of alcohol within two hours and still being capable of skilled motor activities. Likewise, minimisations can be weighed as well. The susceptibility of memory in recall of criminal occurrences is a subject relevant for all witnesses as well, so contemporary reports are particularly useful.

Inconsistencies between the accused and other neutral observers can be evaluated by reviewing these with the accused and seeing what he has to say about the discrepancies.

Chapter 2

The Psychological Assessment

The quality of any opinion that is expressed in a psychological report is only as good as the quality of data that is used to inform that opinion. Apart from information gleaned from interviews and collateral sources, the psychologist is able to draw on a range of different structured assessments. Indeed, the use of tests differentiates the psychologist from other mental health experts.

Choosing the best psychological test to use will depend upon a number of criteria, including its relevance, its validity and reliability, and any constraints related to the testing. This chapter will review a number of standard psychological tests that can assist the psychologist in forming an opinion.

Behaviour During the Assessment

Before beginning the process of testing, it is important to observe the client. Providing a detailed description of that observation is often useful. For example, if the client feels he or she is unable to concentrate or feels uncomfortable with the testing, the results can be affected. The difference between testing a person in a prison (which can be noisy and sometimes fails to provide adequate confidentiality), and testing in a comfortable office may make a crucial difference to the results of the assessment. Equally, accurately describing the person being assessed may be relevant if there are unusual features or characteristics about the way in which he or she presents; for example, if he or she appears overly anxious. A detailed description should include the following elements:

- The information and instructions given to the client prior to commencing the assessment. This should also include outline the explanation provided about the limitations of confidentiality and the purpose of the assessment. For example:
    > At the commencement of the assessment, the nature and purpose of the assessment was explained to the client in the context of a psychological report being prepared for the Court. The limitations of confidentiality were also explained to the client.
- A description of the person can then be provided, including psychological descriptors such as speech behaviour, mood, and rapport. Any

unusual features should be noted, such as whether and when the client was tearful, angry, disconnected, appeared intoxicated or tired.
- Motivation/rapport descriptors (e.g., perceived compliance with requests and co-operation).
- Comprehension of instructions/attention/concentration/effort, and to perceived success/failure/criticism/feedback.
- Details about the date and time and place of the assessment.

Essential Elements of Psychological Tests

As a minimum, any psychological test should have particular psychometric properties. These include that:

- The test is current and in common usage.
- The test has demonstrated validity and reliability.
- Test limitations are clearly identifiable (e.g., age limits, reading level limits).
- Full normative data are available for both clinical and non-clinical populations.
- Administration procedures are clearly defined and standardised.
- A body of literature exists to support the use of the particular test.
- It incorporates a measure of response bias.

In reporting the psychometric data the psychologist should, where possible, include descriptive information about the test, results expressed in relevant comparative terms (e.g., as percentile scores), and a statement about the comparative sample. Sufficient detail should be presented so that another expert can read the report and make relevant inferences. When including psychometric test results in a report it is sometimes helpful to label the headings that define the general area of the assessment (e.g., Cognitive Functioning, Personality Profile, Clinical Profile, Risk Assessment). Each section should then include a statement about the test used, its purpose and a summary of the overall findings. If there is a lot of information about a particular test instrument that needs to be included, then this is best placed in an appendix.

Veracity of Psychological Tests in Court

The validity and reliability of some tests, such as those that purport to measure intelligence, are frequently debated in court. This is a probably a result of to public ignorance about the psychometric data that underpins psychological tests. Sometimes legal counsel will use such ignorance (knowingly or otherwise) to discredit a test by examining specific items of the test and trying to establish that an answer is either misleading, incorrect or lacks relevance. The Wechsler intelligence tests are a frequent target of this attack despite the fact that the profession recognises such instruments are among the best validated tests.

Professional societies have sought to address the issue of how to avoid potential abuse of psychological instruments, however, there appear to be few effective solutions to ensure that the integrity of test materials is protected. While it is often argued that confidentiality and the test copyright would be seriously damaged if a test becomes open to public scrutiny, courts sometimes see this as an irrelevancy and demand the right to examine all technical information without the background to appreciate its qualities. In providing appropriate information to the court it is important to meet the court demands with minimal risk of disclosing sensitive test information, while being mindful that not assisting the court may lead to the psychologist being held in contempt. It is nonetheless appropriate to express reluctance to photocopy materials (stating reasons of copyright protection) and explain the problems likely to be experienced with test interpretation for non-psychologists who are unfamiliar with psychometric test properties. Remember that the psychologist may be bullied and coerced by counsel as a strategy to undermine the evidence if it is not helpful to their case.

Test publishers Harcourt have outlined in a procedure that may be referred to if appropriate:

> Harcourt does not wish to impede the progress of legal proceedings; however, we are equally unwilling to jeopardise the security and integrity of our Test instruments by consenting to the release of copyrighted and confidential material to those not professionally qualified to obtain them. Should litigation in which a psychologist is involved reach the stage where a Court considers ordering the release of propriety Test materials to non-professionals such as counsel, we request that the Court issue a protective order prohibiting parties from making copies of the materials; requiring that the materials be returned to the professional at the conclusion of the proceedings; and requiring that the material not be publicly available as part of the record of the case, whether this is done by sealing part of the record or by not including the materials in the record at all. In addition, testimony regarding the items, particularly that which makes clear the content of the items, should be sealed and again not be included in the record. Pleadings and other documents filed by the parties should not, unless absolutely necessary, make specific reference to the content of or responses to any item, and any proportion of any document that does so, should be sealed. Finally, we ask that the Judge's opinion including both findings of fact and conclusions of law, not include descriptions or quotations of the items or responses. We think this is the minimum requirement to protect our copyright and other propriety rights in the Test, as well as the security and integrity of the Test.

In North America, some test publishers have asked psychologists to release to them the name of the person seeking (or obtaining) test materials through the means of a court order as this is a violation of copyright and could result in legal consequences for that party. Releasing this type of information to counsel or the courts often has the effect of pausing the confrontation and it is then that the alternative is agreed upon. The solution to the request to release raw test material to unauthorised personnel is one which is easy to accomplish, and should be offered to parties early. The party seeking the raw test material can simply retain an independent psychologist to whom the data can be sent and the party can then have a properly filtered buffer who can advise them whether the test was interpreted correctly.

Categories of Psychological Tests

Selecting the appropriate psychological test to use in an assessment is an important skill that can mean the difference between a strong empirically supported report and a weak, poorly justified one. As a general rule, it is sound logic to only make inferences when the data are there to support them. The more relevant the data, the more opportunity there is for the psychologist to evaluate the client accurately, and the more watertight will be the opinion. For example, providing an opinion about a person's intellectual functioning will always have more weight when it is based on the results of a standardised test than it will when based only on clinical judgment.

Psychological tests can be used to determining the client's capacity to perform particular tasks, whether they be cognitive or perceptual, tasks of learning, behavioural tasks, motor skill tasks or developmental tasks. In each of these situations 'performance-based' measures provide data that can be compared with statistical norms and thus indicate an individual's ability relative to comparative sample groups. Determining whether a person has a particular disability may depend specifically on his or her level of performance with a particular test.

Many psychological tests are based upon an individual's self-report, where the assessed person's data are compared with that of a known population sample. This provides information about how the person sees him or herself relative to others, according to defined criteria, which may be personality-based, clinically based, interest-based or behaviourally based. In all cases of self-report data there are implicit biases, which many psychometric tests seek to address through measures of response set or social desirability. These help the psychologist determine the extent to which the subject has provided a valid profile. Typically such measures identify positive or negative impression bias, the level of consistency in responding, and the level of attention the client provides in accurately reading questionnaire material and following instructions.

The Psychological Assessment

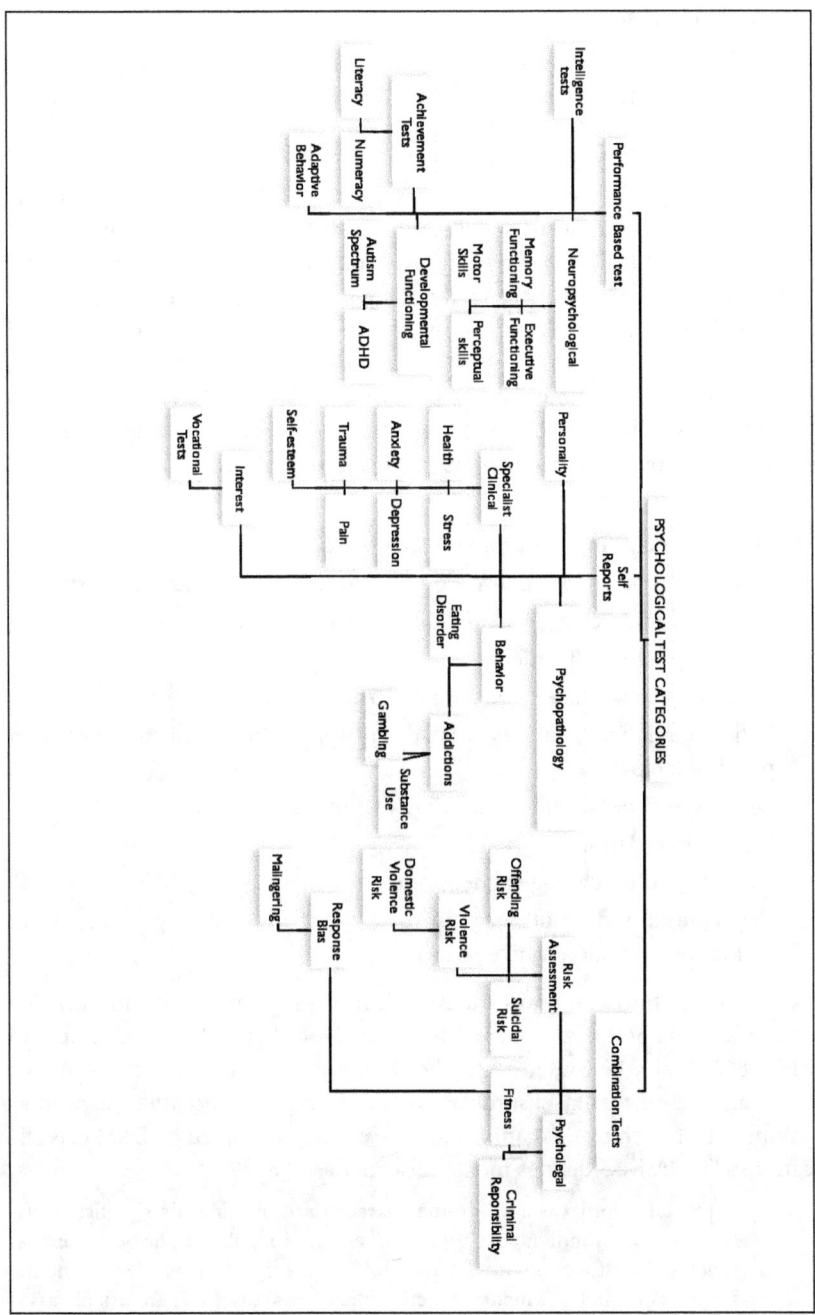

Figure 2.1 Categories of psychological tests.

Assessment of Mental Disorder

One of the major objectives of a psychological report is to determine whether the defendant has a mental disorder. The classification of mental disorders draws on two widely established systems: the World Health Organization's (WHO) International Classification of Diseases (ICD-10) and the American Psychiatric Association's (APA) Diagnostic and Statistical Manual of Mental Disorders. Both systems list categories of disorders that are thought to be distinct types, and have deliberately converged their codes in recent revisions so that the manuals are broadly comparable.

The International Classification of Diseases (ICD) is an international standard diagnostic classification for a wide variety of health conditions. Chapter V focuses on 'mental and behavioural disorders' and consists of 10 main groups. Within each group there are more specific subcategories. The ICD includes personality disorders in the same domain as other mental disorders:

- Organic, including symptomatic, mental disorders
- Mental and behavioural disorders due to use of psychoactive substances
- Schizophrenia, schizotypal and delusional disorders
- Mood [affective] disorders
- Neurotic, stress-related and somatoform disorders
- Behavioural syndromes associated with physiological disturbances and physical factors
- Disorders of personality and behaviour in adult persons
- Mental retardation
- Disorders of psychological development
- Behavioural and emotional disorders with onset usually occurring in childhood and adolescence.

DSM-5 is the fifth edition of the American Psychiatric Association's (APA) *Diagnostic and Statistical Manual of Mental Disorders* and was published on May 18, 2013. In the United States the DSM serves as a primary authority for the diagnosis of mental disorders. Treatment recommendations, as well as payment by health care organisations, are often determined by DSM classifications. The DSM-5 defines mental disorder as:

> A mental disorder is a syndrome characterised by clinically significant disturbance in an individual's cognition, emotion regulation, or behavior that reflects a dysfunction in the psychological, biological, or developmental processes underlying mental functioning. Mental disorders are usually associated with significant distress or disability in social, occupational, or other important activities. An expectable or culturally approved response to a common stressor or loss, such as the death of a loved one, is not a mental

disorder. Socially deviant behavior (e.g., political, religious or sexual) and complex that our primary between the individual and society are not mental disorders unless the deviance or conflict results from a dysfunction in the individual, as described above (p. 20).

Performance Based Tests
Tests of Intellectual Functioning

Information about a person's cognitive functioning can provide considerable assistance in determining not only characteristics about the individual's principal diagnosis, but also information relating to treatment issues and prognosis. When conducting a criminal forensic assessment, time constraints are a fact of life. For this reason it is often appropriate to utilise briefer measures, rather than full tests when establishing the intellectual functioning of the client. If abnormalities are indicated in a preliminary assessment, either more comprehensive intelligence tests (such as the Wechsler Adult Intelligence Scale-Fourth Edition; WAIS–IV) or a selection of neuropsychological tests may be needed or at least recommended within the context of the report. Contemporary tests that provide a measure of a person's intellectual functioning include the following:

- Full version:
    - Stanford-Binet Intelligence Scales, 5th edition (SB5)
    - Wechsler Adult Intelligence Scale, 4th edition (WAIS-IV)
    - Wechsler Intelligence Scale for Children, 4th edition (WISC-IV).

- Short version:
    - Kaufman Brief Intelligence Test, 2nd edition (KBIT-2)
    - Test of Nonverbal Intelligence, 4th edition (TONI-4)
    - Wechsler Abbreviated Scale of Intelligence, 2nd edition (WASI-II).

Neuropsychological Tests

A full neuropsychological assessment involves measuring functioning across a number of different neuropsychological domains. This section cannot provide a comprehensive coverage of neuropsychological assessment, nor discuss the various issues to be considered in conducting such an assessment. To gain this information readers are referred to what are considered to be the leading texts in this area, Lezak et al. (2012), Strauss et al. (2006), or to the chapter on neuropsychological assessment in Groth-Marnat (2009). Forensic neuropsychology has evolved to become very relevant in criminal cases where issues of general competency (or fitness) to stand trial; to plead to a charge; or to offer a confession are raised. Examples of useful contemporary neuropsychological tests include the following:

- Memory – Learning Ability:
  - Memory Assessment Scales (MAS)
  - Wechsler Memory Scale, 4th edition (WMS-IV)

- Visual Spatial Ability
  - Test of Visual-Motor Skills, 3rd Edition (TVMS-3)
  - Test of Visual-Perceptual Skills, 3rd Edition (TVPS-3)
  - Rey Complex Figure Test and Recognition Trial (RCFT)
  - Motor Skills Ability
  - Symbol Digit Modalities Test (SDMT)
  - Test of Visual-Motor Skills, 3rd Edition (TVMS-3)
  - Executive Functioning
  - Stroop Color and Word Test
  - Delis-Kaplan Executive Function System (D-KEFS)
  - Trail Making Test (TMT).

Achievement Tests

Achievement tests aim to measure a person's skill or knowledge of a particular subject or field. They are often contrasted with tests that measure aptitude. Achievement test items include standard items that define a specific level of knowledge. The goal of the test is to measure the skills and knowledge attained and compare that with other performers.

Achievement tests are particularly helpful in determining an individual's level of literacy or numeracy, and general level of academic knowledge. As such, achievement measures can be used to assure the assessor that the client has the requisite ability to complete self-report tests. Examples of relevant achievement tests include:

- General Academic skill
  - Wide Range Achievement Test 4
  - Kaufman Functional Academic Skills Test (K-FAST).

- Literacy skills
  - Progressive Achievement Tests in Reading (PAT-R)
  - Compass Literacy Assessment (CLA).

- Numeracy skills
  - Advanced Numerical Reasoning Appraisal (ANRA)
  - Compass Numeracy Assessment (CAN).

Personality Tests

Objective personality tests measure an individual's typical characteristics, independent of rating bias or the examiner's own beliefs. The results are usually derived from responses to a questionnaire that covers a number of questions scored using standardised methods. Objective tests are very structured and claim much greater validity and reliability than projective tests. Projective tests involve questions that are open-ended and relatively unstructured which give the person being tested more freedom to respond. The responses can be interpreted in various ways. Over recent years, however, projective tests have been strongly criticised for their lack of validity and reliability. Examples of useful personality tests include the following:

- Objective Tests
  - NEO Personality Inventory-Revised (NEO PI-R)
  - 16 Personality Factor Questionnaire (16-PF)
  - Millon Clinical Multiaxial Inventory-III (MCMI-III).

- Projective Tests
  - Thematic Apperception Test (TAT)
  - Rorschach Inkblot Test (RIT)
  - Rorschach Interpretation Assistance Program: Version 5 Forensic Edition (RIAP5 FE).

Test of Psychopathology

One of the first of general tests of psychopathology was the Minnesota Multiphasic Personality Inventory (MMPI), originally developed in 1939 (Hathaway & McKinley, 1940) but updated in 1989 with new normative data and adapted scales. The most recent version is the MMPI-2RF (Ben-Porath & Tellegen, 2011), although its validity and language has been questioned. No longer are terms such as 'hypochrondriasis' or 'psychasthenia' a part of psychological language, but have been replaced by 'somatic complaints' and 'obsessive-compulsive behaviour'.

The Personality Assessment Inventory (PAI), developed by Leslie Morey in 1991, has become the most widely used contemporary test of psychopathology. It represents a new generation of tests that offers greatly improved psychometrics. The PAI adds important new clinical scales and subscales that are particularly relevant to forensic assessments, such as those that assess substance use, posttraumatic stress, as well as borderline and antisocial personality features. 'Treatment' scales include measures of 'aggression', 'suicide ideation', 'stress', 'lack of support' and 'treatment orientation'. These scales help identify problems that may emerge in the context of treatment. Finally, the PAI provides 'interpersonal scales' that measure how the person interacts with others in relation to dimensions of 'dominance' and 'warmth'. The PAI also includes some relatively sophisticated validity scales that measure a client's potential response bias, especially when describing symptoms in terms of exaggeration or underreporting.

A considerable body of literature has now accumulated in relation to using the PAI (e.g., Duellman & Bowers, 2004; Edens, Cruise & Buffington-Vollum, 2001; Edens, Hart, Johnson, Johnson & Olver 2000; Helmes, 1993; White, 1996) and it now appears one of the most significant and important contemporary clinical measures available to the psychologist to aid diagnosis, offender understanding and rehabilitation.

Examples of useful psychopathology tests include:

- Personality Assessment Inventory (PAI)
- Minnesota Multiphasic Personality Inventory-2 Restructured Form (MMPI-2-RF)
- Adolescent Psychopathology Scale (APS)
- Symptom Checklist-90-Revised (SCL-90-R)
- Structured Clinical Interview for DSM-IV Axis 1 (SCID-I) and Axis 2 (SCID-II).

Specialist Clinical Tests

When an assessor wishes to measure specific clinical features, a single dimensional test is often sought. In this context a focus on specific significant symptomatology (e.g., elevated anxiety, depression, traumatic stress) is warranted. Details from specific tests can indicate where the person fits within a known clinical population, and the measure may provide more details about the person's condition.

Often such tests also incorporate the DSM criteria in order to provide clinical checks for a particular mental health diagnostic disorder (e.g., the Posttraumatic Stress Diagnostic Scale). Self-report tests have the potential to be of enormous benefit to the psychologist. An implicit problem with any self-report test, however, is that the test may require a reading and comprehension level beyond that of the person being assessed. Some tests incorporate measures to determine the likelihood of this occurring and it may be necessary to present the information orally. It is also noted that impaired individuals may have more difficulty with questions that are negatively phrased than those that are positively phrased. A useful technique with such questions is to ask the individual the question twice, in both a positive and negative form. If there is an inconsistency in the responses, then seek further clarification. While some argue that any change from the procedure outlined in a test manual invalidates the test, others will contend that it is of greater importance to get essential data that may shed some light upon that person's psychological condition than to have incorrect or no data at all. Examples of specific tests include:

- Health
    - General Health Questionnaire (GHQ)
    - Nottingham Health Profile (NHP)
    - The Short Form (36) Health Survey (SF-36).

- Stress
    - Life Stressors and Social Resources Inventory (LSSRI)
    - Kessler Psychological Distress Scale (K-10)
    - Occupational Stress Inventory-Revised (OSI-R)
    - Depression Anxiety & Stress Scale (DASS).

- Trauma
    - Trauma Symptom Inventory-2 (TSI-2)
    - Detailed Assessment of Post Traumatic Stress (DAPS)
    - Posttraumatic Stress Diagnostic Scale (PDS).

- Pain
    - Psychosocial Pain Inventory (PSPI)
    - The Quebec Back Pain Disability Scale (QBPDS)
    - Brief Pain Inventory (BPI).

- Anxiety
    - Multidimensional Anxiety Questionnaire (MAQ)
    - State–Trait Anxiety Inventory (STAI)
    - Beck Anxiety Inventory (BAI).

- Depression
    - Beck Depression Inventory–II (BDI–II)
    - Clinical Assessment of Depression (CAD)
    - Reynolds Depression Screening Inventory (RDSI).
- Self-Esteem
    - Beck Hopelessness Scale (BHS)
    - Cognitive Distortion Scales (CDS)
    - Multidimensional Self-Esteem Inventory (MSEI).

One of the most significant factors influencing criminal behaviour is substance abuse. This can impact upon criminal behaviour either directly, where the substances influence the criminal behaviour (e.g., violence, risk-taking etc.) or indirectly, where the offender commits an offence (e.g., theft, deception) in order to obtain drugs, to satisfy a substance addiction. Examples of specific substance use tests include:

- Alcohol Use Inventory (AUI)
- Substance Abuse Subtle Screening Inventory (SASSI-3)
- Addiction Severity Index (ASI).

The main measure to assess problem gambling in the community is the Problem Gambling Severity Index of the Canadian Problem Gambling Index. The South Oaks Gambling Screen, which was designed as a clinical measure, is also widely used. Examples of specific gambling addiction tests include:

- Maroondah Assessment Profile for Problem Gambling
- Gambler Addiction Index (GAI)
- Canadian Problem Gambling Index (CPGI)
- South Oaks Gambling Screen (SOGS)
- Victorian Gambling Screen (VGS)
- Problem and Pathological Gambling Measure (PPGM).

Vocational Tests

Vocational tests are tests that are designed to help individuals understand how a variety of personal attributes (i.e., interests, values, preferences, motivations, aptitudes and skills) relate to their potential success and satisfaction with different career options and work environments. Their focus is largely on helping school students determine which subjects they should focus on to reach a chosen career path but they also benefit individuals seeking to change career direction or to open up areas of opportunity not considered previously. In the context of the criminal report, the ability to find employment may be important to successfully reintegration into the community.

Examples of specific tests include:

- Self-Directed Search, 5th Edition Form R (SDS)
- Career Attitudes and Strategies Inventory (CASI)
- Reading-Free Vocational Interest Inventory: 2 (R-FVII:2)
- Vocational Preference Inventory (VPI)
- Assessment of Earning Capacity, 3rd Edition.

Risk Assessment

An opinion relevant to sentencing decisions is one of the most common reasons an expert is asked to assist the court in criminal matters. A judge may find it useful when sentencing a person to have information regarding the offender's risk of recidivism. Methods of predicting who will commit further offences (and who will not) are commonly known as risk assessments. Implicit in any attempt to assess risk is the belief that some individuals are less at risk of committing further offences than others. A considerable amount of research over the last three decades has sought to identify those factors that are associated with offending, although the focus of much of this work is on predicting offending in those known to have committed violent or sexual offences (see Casey, Day, Ward, & Vess, 2012).

Professional methods of assessing risk are typically based on two main tactics, commonly known as the unstructured clinical judgment and the actuarial approaches. Clinical predictions of risk primarily involve idiosyncratic clinical judgments about an individual's likelihood of re-offending based upon a practitioner's knowledge of that individual and their own experiences. The actuarial approach involves assessing risk solely on the basis of the statistical probability that offenders with a particular set of characteristics will re-offend. Predictions are based on empirically established correlations between a risk measure (typically based on known characteristics of both the offender and the offence) and recidivism of groups having those characteristics. A third method, referred to as structured professional judgment employs a checklist of pre-determined risk factors that have been selected from the empirical research. While the judgment of risk is still based on the clinical view of the evaluator, it is guided by a structured set of reliable parameters that are considered in the final opinion of risk

There has been considerable, and at times heated, debate between practitioners and researchers about the value of each approach, but there appears to now be a consensus that structured approaches to risk assessment should be used, given concerns that purely clinical approaches to risk assessment possess inadequate reliability and predictive validity. This means that unstructured clinical assessments of risk are not only likely to be less accurate that actuarial and structured professional judgment assessments, but also that different assessors are more likely to reach different conclusions. Nonetheless, clinical judgment is still important in highlighting particular factors associated with the individual case that are identified as important.

A common approach is to use actuarial risk assessment tools (where available) to obtain a probabilistic estimate of recidivism and also follow structured guidelines to identify areas of risk that can be managed, to inform an opinion. In other words, start by establishing the likely probability of an individual with particular characteristics re-offending within a specified time frame and then consider those dynamic risk factors which may impact on his or her ability to desist. These would include substance use, association with anti-social or offending peers, current attitudes and beliefs about offending, social support and so on.

One particular difficulty arises in knowing how to interpret a risk score obtained on an actuarial risk assessment measure in cases where the assessed person has no previous history of offending. Risk assessment tools have been developed on the basis of the characteristics of known offenders who are subsequently re-convicted of further offences. Actuarial risk assessment tools have not generally been developed or validated for use with people who have not previously offended and as such caution must be applied when using such assessments with this group. Examples of offender risk of general offending measures include:

- Inventory of Offender Risk, Needs, and Strengths (IORNS)
- PAI Interpretive Report for Correctional Settings (PAI-CS)
- Psychosocial Evaluation & Threat Risk Assessment (PETRA)
- Risk-Sophistication-Treatment Inventory (RSTI)
- Level of Service/Case Management Inventory (LSI-R)
- General Statistical Information on Recidivism (GSIR).

It has been established that the risk factors for general re-offending differ substantially from those that predict violent offending. As such it is usually recommended that these general risk assessment be augmented with those that specifically assess risk of violence when violent offending is present. These typically assess specific risk factors such as attempted strangulation, imminent or recent separation, and/or victim beliefs regarding the offender's likelihood of killing the victim/children (see Messing & Thaller, 2013), and may utilise information about risk from victims.

- Classification of Violence Risk (COVR)
- Historical Clinical Risk -20, Version 3 (HCR-20 V3)
- State-Trait Anger Expression Inventory–2 (STAXI-2)
- Anger Disorder Scale (ADS)
- Violent Risk Appraisal Guide (VRAG)
- Spousal Assault Risk Assessment Guide (SARA)
- Sexual Violence Risk-20 (SVR-20)
- Sex Offender Risk Appraisal Guide (SORAG)
- Static-99 & Static 2002
- Psychopathy Check List – Revised (PCL-R)
- Rapid Risk Assessment for Sex Offence Recidivism (RRASOR)
- Minnesota Sex Offender Screening Tool - Revised (MnSORT-R).

Availability of Treatment or Rehabilitation

Offender rehabilitation programs that are typically offered are usually delivered to groups over a specified number of sessions and target either specific offence categories or what have been termed 'criminogenic needs' or dynamic risk factors. In matters involving sentencing, it is important that the report provide details regarding:

- Whether or not the person has previously engaged in rehabilitation programs
- The nature and duration of any rehabilitation programs
- The client's perception of the programs in changing his or her behaviour
- Whether the programs were aimed at adolescents or adults
- What is the client's level of willingness and motivation to participate in future programs recommended by the court (should that be an option)
- What rehabilitation programs are available
- Whether the client has special needs (e.g., low literacy skills).

Suicide risk assessment may also be relevant to sentencing matters. This type of assessment should clearly distinguish between acute and chronic risk. Acute risk might be raised because of recent changes in the person's circumstances or mental state, while chronic risk is determined by a diagnosis of a mental illness, and social and demographic factors. Risk factors for prison self-harm and suicide can be grouped into four categories: personal, contextual, historical, and clinical risk factors. Personal risk factors are the characteristics of the individual, including stable aspects of the person, such as age and gender or personality traits and dispositions, and state factors such as their response to recent stresses, or problems adjusting to imprisonment. Stressful events include threats to personal relationships, domestic problems, loss events and a variety of stressors associated with prison life such as bullying, intimidation, isolation and disturbing psychological symptoms.

Prisoners who are held on remand have consistently higher self-harm rates than those who have been convicted and sentenced. There is consistent evidence that self-harm rates are higher within the first week of imprisonment and this may be a result of feelings of trauma, isolation, separation, shame, and embarrassment. Other relevant factors to consider include a recurrence of psychiatric symptoms, or drug withdrawal. A substantial proportion of prisoners who self-harm are dependent upon narcotics prior to incarceration. Contemporary measures of suicide risk include:

- Adult Suicidal Ideation Questionnaire (ASIQ)
- Beck Suicide Inventory (BSI)
- Suicidal Ideation Questionnaire (SIQ)
- Firestone Assessment of Self-Destructive Thoughts (FAST)
- Firestone Assessment of Suicide Intent (FASI)
- Adult Suicidal Ideation Questionnaire (ASIQ)
- PTSD and Suicide Screener (PSS).

Impression Management and Malingering

Nesca and Dalby (2013) wrote that:

> All forensic interviews must begin with the assumption that the interviewee is motivated to lie or distort information and, as a result, cannot be completely trusted. But in sifting through the data provided by the patient, how do you tell the truth from a lie, a misrepresentation, or an exaggeration of essentially truthful facts? It is not the role of the forensic examiner to guarantee that the information he or she has extracted from the patient is truthful. But should forensic interviewers make efforts to encourage patients to be honest or just take them and their information as they come? (p.40)

So how can the assessor objectively determine the likely response bias of a client? One increasingly important approach is the use of psychometric tools that assess response bias. In its simplest form these measures determine an individual's bias towards seeing him or herself in a more positive light (and more socially desirable than reality would indicate) or seeing him or herself in a more negative light (with more negative problems than is actually the case). A person wishing to appear impaired for some reason may aim to exaggerate negative clinical symptoms, while a person wishing to present without any problems may exaggerate a favorable self-image. Tests that incorporate response bias measures include:

- Personality Assessment Inventory (PAI; NIM PIM scales and others)
- Minnesota Multiphasic Personality Inventory, 2nd Edition; Lie (L), Infrequency (F), and Correction (K) scales
- Millon Clinical Multiaxial Inventory-III (MCMI-III) Disclosure (X), Desirability (Y), Debasement (Z), Validity (V) and Inconsistency (W).

Malingering is the purposeful production of false or grossly exaggerated symptoms with the goal of receiving a reward or benefit that may be money, an insurance settlement, drugs or the avoidance of punishment, work, jury duty, military or some other kind of service. A malingerer may respond to items in a certain manner to obtain a perceived profile that he or she believes will enable them to receive a beneficial outcome. Tests of malingering have evolved with some sophistication, beyond just showing a response bias with the subject's responding. One group of measures was developed by identifying individuals whose responses were outside the 'normal' clinical response set. For example, the Structured Interview of Reported Symptoms (SIRS; Rogers et al., 1992) was originally developed to detect malingering of mental illness. The original SIRS comprised of 172 items divided among 8 primary scales assessing rare symptoms, improbable and absurd symptoms, symptom combinations, blatant symptoms, subtle symptoms, symptom severity, symptom selectivity, and reported versus observed symptoms. Each scale provides four categorisations: honest, indeterminate, probable faking, and definite faking. An updated version of the SIRS, SIRS-2 provides an expanded scoring and classification, to assess deliberate distortions in the self-report of symptoms. Each scale produces useful information on how a particular client may distort or fabricate his or her symptoms. The primary focus of the SIRS-2 is on the evaluation of feigning and the manner in which it is likely to occur—for example, exaggeration of symptom severity versus fabrication of symptomatology. Malingering self-report measures include:

- Self Report Structured Inventory of Malingered Symptomatology (SIMS)
- Miller Forensic Assessment of Symptoms Test (M-FAST)
- Trauma Symptom Inventory-2 (TSI-2)
- Structured Interview of Reported Symptoms, 2nd Edition (SIRS-2)
- Victoria Symptom Validity Test (VSVT)
- Personality Assessment Inventory (PAI) (MAL scale).

Various neuropsychology measures of malingering have been developed to distinguish subjects whose responses are well outside the expected normative performance range. These tests usually involve memory tasks. Subjects are instructed that the task is relatively difficult, when in fact, it normative data shows it to be relatively easy. Those without severe and obvious memory impairments who performed poorly on such tests are suspected of faking pathology. Such a measure is most relevant in criminal cases where the accused offers a cognitive disability as a defense. These tests include:

- Test of Memory Malingering (TOMM)
- Rey 15 Item Test (15-IT)
- Validity Indicator Profile (VIP).

Psycho-Legal Tests

One of the most important assessment functions of an expert witness is associated with determining whether an individual has the capacity, due to his or her mental impairment, to engage in the legal process, or to satisfy rules of law relating to guilt.

Fitness or Competency Tests

Expert witnesses evaluate a client's fitness to stand trial using interviews, empirical tools, psychometrics, behavioural indicators and legal standards. In making a determination of mental impairment and its relationship to fitness/competency, the complexity of the evidence and the likely nature of proceedings are taken into account. Specialised fitness/competency measures are often used by psychologists to assist them form an opinion, and to provide and important guide to examining pertinent issues.

Fitness assessment instruments have been considered by some to be more reliable than professional judgment alone when assessing baseline competencies. However, fitness criteria are usually defined in terms of abilities, and therefore psychologists evaluate the person's demonstration of relevant competencies using observations and behavioural measures (e.g., ratings based on the person's behaviour during police interviews and other analogous settings to what will be required of the person throughout the legal process or in court). It is particularly important for the assessor to demonstrate how the specifics of the defendant's mental impairment relate to specific deficits defined in the relevant legislation. Common standardised psychometric tools for measuring fitness (or 'competency') [US]) include:

- Evaluation of Competency to Stand Trial–Revised (ECST-R)
- MacArthur Competence Assessment Tool-Criminal Adjudication (MacCAT-CA)
- Fitness Interview Test (FIT).

Criminal Responsibility Tests

A structured test to assess a person's 'criminal responsibility' or 'insanity' aims to provide an operational measure of critical legal criteria (e.g., McNaughton Rules) and apply it to the psychological phenomena. The advantage of such testing is that it ensures the assessor provides a thorough assessment of all relevant criteria in a systematic way.

Rogers' development of the Criminal Responsibility Assessment Scales (R-CRAS) provided a criterion based decision model for criminal responsibility based on the American Law Institute Standard of Insanity, the McNaughton Standard of Insanity and the Guilty But Mentally Ill standard. The R-CRAS is not a formal psychological test and is not administered to the defendant. Rather, it provides a protocol for organising and quantifying key symptomatology. Ratings of severity are keyed to the time of the offence and related to the alleged criminal behaviour.

CHAPTER 3

Opinion

In the following chapter, five different types of court report are provided to illustrate the way in which an expert witness might communicate the results of his or her assessment to the court. When reading the reports consider the different styles and similarities between them. All names have been altered, as has any identification of associated parties.

Mr Jack Jones
Background to the Case
This is an interesting Australian case involving the crime of child pornography, taking into account the extent to which the defendant's mental health should be considered a mitigating factor in sentencing. Mr Jones was facing charges of 'Possession of Child pornography' and 'Using a Carriage Service to access Child Pornography'. He was referred by his defence lawyer for a psychological assessment. The lawyer also asked for an opinion on whether Mr Jones was incompetent (or legally insane) at the time of the offending.

After the judge had determined the sentence, the defendant appealed the severity of the sentence. Subsequently a higher court judge ruled not to uphold the appeal, and the legal arguments were explained in his findings.

Background History
Personal History
Mr Jones stated that he was born in Fundon on 6 August 1969, and is now aged 42 years. Mr Jones said that his parents had separated in 1984 when he was aged 15 years and was uncertain as to whether or not his father was still alive. Mr Jones said that he was not distressed when his parents separated, as he believed they had only stayed together '*to make me happy*'.

Mr Jones indicated that he was largely raised by his maternal grandparents. He said his maternal grandmother died in 2005 and was '*a very strong person*', with whom Mr Jones said he had '*a very close*' relationship. He said he was still dealing with the loss of his grandmother. Mr Jones stated that his grandfather died in 1978. He said his grandfather was '*a very lovely and kind man*', whom he also felt '*very close*' to. He said he coped poorly with his grandfather's death.

Mr Jones stated that his mother was now aged 73 years and living in Fundon. He described her as *'an evil and nasty person who was extremely manipulative'*. He said his mother had been a very heavy drinker, and had never worked in paid employment. He said, *'she has mental problems'*. Mr Jones stated that his relationship with his mother was *'non-existent'* and that he last had contact with her in 2005 (by telephone).

Mr Jones said that his mother had always told him that he *'was a mistake and should have been a girl'*.

Mr Jones said that his father was now aged 76 years, and was *'a quiet, mean man'*, who was living in Europe. Mr Jones said that the last time he had contact with his father was in 1984, when his parents separated. He said that even when his parents were together he rarely saw his father, who was often working nightshift in a factory.

Mr Jones said that his general childhood memories were happy, and he particularly enjoyed playing with the children next door. He said his favourite times were going on holidays with his grandmother, or working with his grandparents in the market garden. He said his saddest memory was associated with his grandfather's death.

Mr Jones said that prior to his birth, his mother had a daughter, who had died from blood poisoning aged around 2 months. Mr Jones said that although his mother did not speak about this, it had clearly had a significant impact upon her. Mr Jones said that he also had a maternal half-brother, John, who was now aged 57 years, and also living in Adelaide. He said his brother was divorced and worked in a landscape business. Mr Jones said that his relationship with his half-brother was *'non-existent'*.

Mr Jones indicated that he was currently married to Nadia, who was 15 years younger than he and with whom he had been in a relationship with since 2009. He said that they married on 19 October 2011. He described their relationship as *'wonderful'* and that his partner was *'a very kind, generous and understanding person'*, who worked as a personal carer and was trained as a nurse. He said that she gave him great support. Mr Jones said they did not have any children together.

Mr Jones said that he had previously been in a relationship with Pamela from 1997 to 2003. Mr Jones said that he had thought the relationship was *'fine'* but did not realise she had a significant gambling problem. He said his former partner was *'a very sly and bitter person'* and that the relationship ended after she had an affair. Mr Jones stated that they had one child together, a daughter Ann-Marie (born 12 July 1998). Mr Jones said that his 12-year-old daughter was *'a very happy child'*, who was living interstate with her mother. He said that she was currently in Year 8 at school and that he had regular contact with her by telephone twice a week. He said that his daughter also stayed with him during school holidays and that their relationship was *'very close'*. He said he last spoke by telephone with his daughter two days previous, and last had contact with her face-to-face around Christmas 2010.

Mr Jones stated that he was currently living in a rented two bedroomed unit in Adelaide with his wife. He said he had been living there for the past 4 months and was relatively happy there, although he was concerned that it was *'very noisy'*.

Education

Mr Jones stated that he had completed his education to Year 12 level. He said that he attended Market Junior Primary School (Reception – Year 3) and Frankston Primary School (Year 4–Year 7). He said he was *'unhappy'* as a student at primary school, and had few friends. Mr Jones indicated that he then attended Mansfield Agricultural High School (Year 8–Year 12).

Mr Jones said that academically in primary school his performance was *'below average'* and had repeated Year 4. He said that his mother told him at the time, *'I was stupid, slow and an idiot like my father'*. He said that he was never in trouble at primary school. He said he was *'very happy'* as a student at secondary school, and had many friends. Mr Jones said that academically in secondary school his performance was *'average'* and his favourite subjects were Horticulture and Business Mathematics. He said that he was never in trouble at secondary school. He brought in an old school report which confirmed this account. Mr Jones said that he was 18 years old when he left school.

Vocational History

Mr Jones indicated after leaving school he worked in horticulture for himself, Jones' Market Gardening (1988–1992). He said this involved growing salad onions, spinach, and celery. Mr Jones said that he then worked for a celery grower (R.M. Williams & Sons) working as a general farmhand. He said he then moved interstate to care for his grandmother (2001) before returning to Fundon and commencing a new business, which was largely a landscaping business. He said the business ran for approximately 11 months before a back injury forced him to stop working. He said he had not worked since 2003, and had been on Disability Pension since 2005.

Health

Mr Jones indicated that his physical health was *'stable'* and stated that he had a major injury in 2001 when he was hit by a post planting machine, which resulted in him breaking ribs, his hip and knee, and being knocked out. He said that at the time he spent seven days in hospital. He said he did not make a full recovery from the injuries, with 30% residual disability determined.

Mr Jones indicated that he currently saw a regular doctor, Dr Duong and was currently taking a number of prescribed medications that included: Naprosyn SR 1000 (for arthritis), Seroquel (bipolar/depressive disorder), Cymbalta (antidepressant), Inderal (migraine headache), Nitrolingual Spray (Heart), Zydol SR 200 (pain), Stilnox (sleep), and Ventolin (breathing). Dr Duong was contacted and confirmed that this was true. Mr Jones rated his current physical health at 4/10. He said that in the past the best it had been was 8/10, the worst 2/10 (in 2001).

Mental Health

Mr Jones indicated that his mental health was '*not good*'. He said his main stressors were associated with his Court matters, and the realisation of the seriousness of his charges. Mr Jones said that in the past he had been diagnosed with depression and bipolar disorder, and that he had also experienced psychotic symptoms. He said he was seeing a psychiatrist, Dr Knighton (2004-2005), and a report prepared by Dr Knighton (21 February 2005) stated:

> In my opinion, Mr Jones has been suffering from double depression, that is having a super imposing major depressive disorder on top of a long-standing background of dysthymia (moderate severe depression) (p. 1).

Mr Jones indicated that he had never been happy in his life, but that his mood was now stable and that he did not have problems with anger. Mr Jones said that in the past he had been a victim of emotional abuse (from his mother) and sexual abuse (aged 14 years) from his half-brother, who Mr Jones said was aged 29 years at the time. Mr Jones said that his half-brother had taken him fishing and had raped him during the outing. Mr Jones said that he reported the incident to his family doctor, Dr Gerome Shinks, who apparently said, '*These things can cause a lot of trouble and it is best to forget about it*'. Mr Jones said that he also told his grandmother (who believed him and said, '*it did not surprise her*') and his mother who said that she did not believe him and called him '*a poisonous liar*'.

Mr Jones stated that he had attempted to take his own life on two occasions in 2003 when he took an overdose of pills, and on another occasion with a plastic bag around his head. Mr Jones said that he currently rated his mental health at 4/10. He said that in the past the best had been was 8/10, the worst 1/10.

Substance Use

Mr Jones said that he first drank alcohol at age 17 years. Mr Jones said that he was '*a heavy*' drinker, and predominantly drank beer. He said he would binge drink in order to help himself relax and sleep. He said his drinking was usually after he had finished work, and that he last drank heavily 2 weeks previous. Mr Jones said that he first abused benzodiazepine (Valium) in 2001. He said he continued to use it up until 2009. He said he would often take a week's supply of Valium in 2 nights. Mr Jones denied abusing other substances including cannabis, methamphetamine, ecstasy, cocaine, heroin, hallucinogenic drugs (e.g., LSD), morphine and methadone.

Gambling

Mr Jones said he had a gambling problem, which first started when he was aged 35 years, playing the slot machines. He reported that the frequency of his gambling was 2 to 3 times a week. He said that he last gambled around December 2005 and would lose around $5000 over a 2-month period.

Current Criminal Charges

Mr Jones indicated that he had no prior history of offending. It was indicated that Mr Jones was facing charges of Possession of Child Pornography and Using a Carriage Service to access Child Pornography. He said that at the time he was living alone and was '*mentally unwell*'. He said he felt abandoned by his psychiatrist, and was trying to manage his medication. He said he was also drinking heavily. Mr Jones said at the time he did not know why he was looking at the child pornography, but acknowledged that he got some sexual gratification from seeing it. He said he was mainly interested in '*normal*' pornography, and found that it was a challenge to look for more extreme examples of pornography. He said that searching the internet for pornography became '*a way of filling in time*'. Mr Jones said that when he saw images of children he '*did not see it as a child*'. He said that at the time he did not appreciate its illegality. He said, '*I was alone in a dark room with the door locked*'. He said '*I did not care about most things … I was sick of life*'. Mr Jones said that over time his intensity for looking at extreme material increased ('*it was free*') and that he got excited finding it.

Mr Jones said that at the time he was also having difficulty with his community housing group and experienced conflict with a mentally disturbed patient who was his neighbour.

Rehabilitation History

Mr Jones stated that he had attended a community sex offender treatment program from November 2008 through to 2009. Program staff were able to corroborate this, reporting that he left the program prematurely without successfully completing all of the core content. He said that during the treatment he felt frustrated, because he was a voluntary patient, and they did not make a distinction between '*hands-on offenders*' and those who accessed child pornography. Mr Jones said that at the time he felt sick about the hands-on offender issues, and finally found it too difficult to write about himself in the context of a hands-on offender.

Assessment

Behaviour During Assessment

Mr Jones presented as a 42-year-old Caucasian male of average height and build. He had a fair complexion and was clean-shaven. He had a balding head and wore dark rimmed prescription glasses. He wore a white pin-striped business shirt and dark trousers. He did not wear any jewellery nor did he have visible tattoos or piercings on his person.

Mr Jones was polite and cooperative throughout the assessment and did not appear to have any difficulty understanding the questions asked. The assessment took place at Black and Associates offices on the 25 November 2011, between 11.30 am and 2.30 pm.

Cognitive Functioning

The Complex Figure test was administered in order to assess Mr Jones' ability to organise and plan visual spatial information. This test also provides an indication of the person's higher order processing. Despite producing an accurate copy (see Figure 3.1), Mr Jones' strategy score of 1/6 with this task indicated a limited planning strategy, and a possibility of brain impairment.

The Kaufman Brief Intelligence Test (K-BIT) is a well-developed psychological test that provides an indication of both a person's verbal and non-verbal intelligence, and provides an overall measure of global intelligence. The instrument is well standardised, based on extensive sampling in the

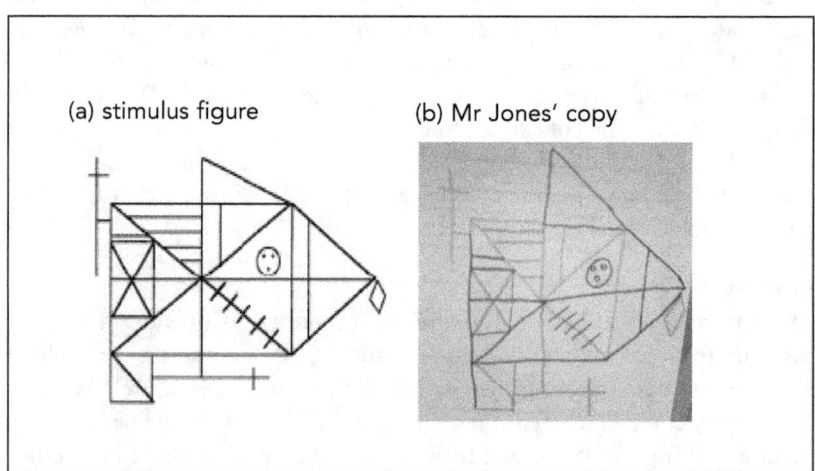

Figure 3.1 Picture taken of Mr Jones' copy of the stimulus figure associated with the Complex Figure test.

United States and Australia, and has been adapted for an Australian population. The results indicated that Mr Jones was in the 'Low Average' (80 < IQ < 90) range of intelligence and around the 19th percentile of the age equivalent population. Mr Jones' verbal IQ was around the 27th percentile while his non-verbal IQ was around the 18th percentile. There was no significant difference between his verbal and nonverbal abilities.

Personality Profile

The revised NEO Personality Inventory (Form S) was used to measure Mr Jones' personality using a dimensional approach. The instrument is a standardised self-report measure, which allows the clinician to measure personality traits that characterise the individual and provide information, which can assist the assessment of likely responsiveness to treatment and prognosis prediction.

Mr Jones' 'personality' profile indicated that he was within the high range for the 'Neuroticism' (N) factor score; within the average range for the 'Openness' (O) and 'Agreeableness' (A) factor scores ; and within the low range for the 'Extraversion' (E) and 'Conscientiousness' (C) factor scores. Such a personality profile indicates that Mr Jones is a person who is emotionally unstable and experiences high levels of anxiety, self-consciousness, and depression. He presents as a generally a distant and cold person who prefers the company of a few rather than many. Mr Jones is open about his feelings and conservative with his ideas. He has limited trust in other people and tends to be stubborn and set in his ways. Mr Jones does not see himself as particularly competent or achievement driven, and is inclined not to be deliberate in completing tasks. He nevertheless sees himself as disciplined, organised, and dutiful.

Clinical Profile

The Personality Assessment Inventory (PAI) was used to objectively assess aspects of Mr Jones' mental health. The PAI is a standardised self-report questionnaire that provides a profile of a person based on his or her responses to items that examine aspects of a person's behaviour and thinking. The measure includes four primary sets of scales: validity scales, clinical scales, treatment scales, and interpersonal scales. The instrument has been normed with a census–matched standardisation sample ($N = 1,000$), college sample ($N = 1051$), clinical sample ($N = 1,246$) and public safety sample group ($N = 17,757$).

Mr Jones' responses were generally consistent, and suggest that he did adopt an overly positive or overly negative response set to the questions. Mr Jones' clinical profile indicated he was elevated on measures of Conversion Symptoms, Somatisation, Anxiety (all scales), Traumatic Stress, Cognitive–

Depression, Affective–Depression, Hypervigilance, Resentment, Schizophrenia (all scales), Identity Problems, Negative Relationships, Antisocial Behaviour, and Alcohol Problems (see Figure 3.2)

Mr Jones' generally elevated clinical profile suggests he experiences considerable psychological dysfunction. He is a person with significant thinking and concentration problems, accompanied by prominent agitation and distress. He is likely to be withdrawn and isolated, with few, if any, close interpersonal relationships, and may become quite anxious and threatened by such relationships. His social judgement is very poor, and he tends to have marked difficulty making decisions, even about matters of little significance.

Mr Jones reported having a significant history of alcohol problems and was unhappy and pessimistic. His drinking may have led to severe impairment in his ability to maintain his social role expectations, and his drinking behaviour had alienated him from many of the people who were once central to his life. He is likely to have experienced setbacks, which had led him to feel significant guilt. He also tends to ruminate negatively about his life circumstances. Such ruminations create more anxiety, which he felt leads him to drink more. When under the influence of alcohol, Mr Jones is likely to be significantly impaired in his judgement.

Mr Jones' PAI treatment profile was significantly elevated on the 'Suicidal Ideation' and 'Non-Support' scales. As Mr Jones' scores on the suicide ideation scale was elevated, the PAI Suicide Potential Index (SPI) scale was

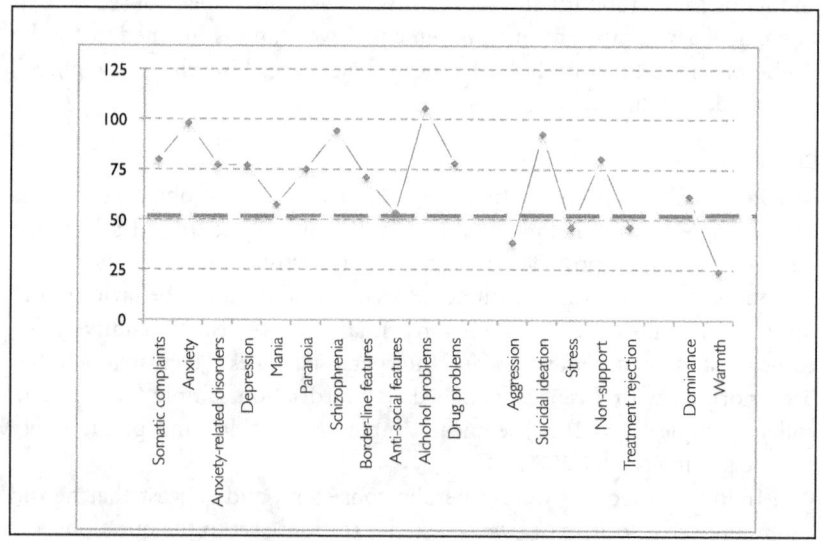

Figure 3.2 Mr Jones' clinical profile (compared with the community normative data [T = 50]).

applied to assess the level of acute risk. This measure included 20 independent, statistically derived measures that are normed against both a community and clinical sample. Mr Jones' score (SPI = 15/20) indicates that compared with the community sample he is in the high-risk group (t score > 80); and for the clinical norm sample is in the moderate risk band (60 < t score < 73). The treatment profile thus indicates that Mr Jones experiences significant thoughts of suicide, and presents a high risk for engaging in suicidal behaviour. He also perceived that he had limited support from family and friends.

On the interpersonal scales (which assess the way a person relates to others), Mr Jones scored high on the 'Dominance' scale and very low on the 'Warmth' scale. Mr Jones' interpersonal style is best characterised as remote and egocentric. Mr Jones is not likely to be interested or invested in social relationships and, as a result, his relationships are likely to be pragmatic and viewed in terms of their potential benefits rather than as sources of enjoyment. Others were likely to view Mr Jones as harsh and punitive and he tended to be sceptical of close relationships and he is likely to avoid commitment if possible.

Problem Gambling

The Maroondah Assessment Profile for Problem Gambling was used to examine the nature of Mr Jones' gambling problem. This instrument was developed in Australia and comprises measures of the individual's beliefs, feelings, situations, self-attitudes and social orientation towards gambling. The gambling profile indicates that Mr Jones is a person for whom gambling greatly influences his feelings. Generally gambling lifts his mood, and he gains some level of relaxation from it, and believes it helps him to control stress levels. Mr Jones also perceived that gambling alleviated his boredom and provided an escape from the perceived demands of other people in his life. At times, Mr Jones experiences a sense of desperation about his financial circumstances and a feeling of being rebellious when gambling.

Opinion

What is Mr Jones' Psychological Status?

Mr Jones' indicated that his parents separated when he was aged around 15 years, and that his relationship with his mother was extremely poor. He said that he was largely raised by his maternal grandparents, with whom he had a positive relationship and he was deeply distressed when his maternal grandfather died when he was aged around 9 years. At the age of 14, Mr Jones reported that he was sexually abused by his 29-year-old half-brother, and was left feeling frustrated and angry when he was not believed by his mother.

Mr Jones said that he completed his education to Year 12 level, and subsequently worked as a market gardener until he was injured in a work accident in 2001, when a stump planter malfunctioned, breaking his ribs and hips. He said the accident put him in hospital for seven days. He said that he did not recover fully from the injuries, and today had significant arthritis as well as ongoing pain related to the injuries.

Mr Jones said that he had always been an unhappy child, and had been diagnosed with depression/bipolar disorder in adulthood. He said that he had been treated by a psychiatrist with medication, and also experienced psychotic symptoms (auditory hallucinations). Mr Jones stated that in 2003 following the breakup of a long-term relationship he attempted to commit suicide, and again in 2007 he was highly suicidal. Mr Jones indicated that he is currently in a very positive relationship, and has been in that relationship since 2009. He said that he had married his 27-year-old partner one-week previous and that she was extremely supportive and caring towards him. Mr Jones said that he had a history of abusing alcohol from the age of 17 years, and also a history of gambling addiction. Mr Jones stated that he had attended a sex offender rehabilitation program in 2008/2009 as a voluntary client, but that he withdrew from that program when they insisted on treating him the same way that they treated 'hands-on' offenders.

The psychological profile indicated that Mr Jones was a person of low average intelligence, who functions around the 19th percentile of the age equivalent population. Preliminary neuropsychological data suggested possible problems with his planning processes and his personality profile indicates that he is generally emotionally unstable, introverted, lacking trust in others, non-compliant and lacking conscientiousness. The clinical profile indicates Mr Jones experiences a range of mental health symptoms. He is interpersonally dominant and low in warmth.

Based on the background history provided by Mr Jones and the psychological testing, a range of the *Diagnostic and Statistical Manual of Mental Disorders* (5th Edition; DSM-5) diagnostic hypotheses can be advanced that include:

- Alcohol Use Disorder (refer DSM-5, pp. 490–497)
- Generalised Anxiety Disorder (refer DSM-5, pp. 189–264)
- Posttraumatic Stress Disorder (refer DSM-5, pp. 271–280)
- Adjustment Disorder with Mixed Depressed Mood (refer DSM-5, pp. 286–289)
- Schizophrenia (refer DSM-5, pp. 99–105)
- Borderline Personality Disorder (refer DSM-5, pp. 663–666).

What is the Relationship Between His Psychological Condition and the Offending?

Mr Jones is facing charges of 'Possession of Child Pornography' and 'Using a Carriage Service to access Child Pornography'. At the time he was living alone and reported being 'mentally unwell'. He said he felt abandoned by his psychiatrist, and was trying to manage his medication. He said he was also drinking heavily. Mr Jones said that at the time he did not know why he was looking at the child pornography, but acknowledged that he got some sexual gratification from seeing it. He said searching the internet for pornography became '*a way of filling in time*'. Mr Jones said that when he saw images of children he '*did not see it as 'a child*'' and did not appreciate its illegality. Mr Jones said that over time his intensity for looking at extreme material increased ('*it was free*') and that he got excited finding it. Mr Jones said that during 2007 to 2008 he was also having difficulty with his community housing group and experienced conflict with a mentally disturbed patient, who was his neighbour.

From a psychological perspective, there is good evidence to suggest that individuals who experience significant depressive symptoms can readily find themselves absorbed in pornography as a means of mood distraction and short-term pleasure. This activity soon becomes highly addictive, where the challenge becomes focused on finding more and more extreme material. In my opinion, Mr Jones was using the internet in this way. He reported closing himself away in a darkened, locked room, and became immersed in pornography, some of which was child pornography. He became more focused on finding extreme pornographic images. By accessing such a large amount of material he became conditioned to their features and only by searching for more and more extreme material did he find gratification. His highly addictive nature was also reflected in his past abuse of alcohol (1986–present) and gambling (2005).

Does Mr Jones Satisfy the Mental Impairment Criteria?

To examine this question, it first necessary to determine whether or not your client has a mental impairment as defined in the legislation. According to section 269a of the local legislation this would include:

   a. A mental illness
   b. An intellectual disability, or
   c. A disability or impairment of the mind resulting from senility.

The assessment indicated that Mr Jones satisfied these criteria for a) Mental illness as he experienced strong depressive feelings and emotional negativity. In relation to the question of 'competency' as defined by the legislation (section 269c) the person is considered to be mentally incompetent if, as a result of his or her mental impairment, the person either:

a. Commits an offence and does not understand the nature of the offence, or
b. Commits an offence, and does not understand the offence was wrong, or
c. Commits an offence and was unable to control the conduct because of the mental impairment.

On the basis of Mr Jones' reporting, it is apparent he understands the nature of his behaviour and understands it to be something of questionable legality (as indicated by his secretive nature, locking the doors etc.). Similarly, it would appear that Mr Jones had the capacity to understand that what he was doing was probably morally wrong, but may not necessarily have understood the full extent of its illegality. Mr Jones struggled with controlling his behaviour with addictions to gambling, alcohol, and pornography. It is unlikely however that this level of control would meet the necessary threshold of 'unable to control the conduct because of his mental health state'. In short, Mr Jones is unlikely to fit the criteria for mental incompetence.

What Rehabilitation Is Recommended to Reduce the Risk of Re-Offending?

The assessment indicated Mr Jones has psychological problems in areas of pain management, anxiety, traumatic stress, depression, paranoia and schizophrenic symptoms. It is therefore recommended that Mr Jones be referred to an appropriate mental health professional (psychiatrist) to address these issues. It is also noted that Mr Jones experiences significant suicidal thoughts, and his risk of potential suicide was judged to be high. Were he to be incarcerated appropriate management strategies would likely need to be put into place to manage this risk.

The assessment indicated that Mr Jones has addiction problems with alcohol, gambling and pornography usage. It is likely that there is a common theme involving Mr Jones' responses to heightened emotional states and his use of addictive behaviours. In my opinion, Mr Jones would benefit from seeing an experienced clinical and forensic psychologist to address these problems in a structured logical way. Given his past experience with the community sex offender treatment program, it is unlikely that he would benefit from this program.

Court Outcome

Mr Jones pleaded guilty to the offences of aggravated possession of child pornography contrary to s 63A(1) of the *Criminal Law Consolidation Act 1935* (SA) and using a carriage service to access child pornography contrary to s 474.19(1)(a)(i) of the *Criminal Code 1995* (Cwlth). The sentencing judge ordered that the two terms of imprisonment be served concurrently – resulting in a total term of imprisonment of 18 months with a non-parole period of 12 months imposed for the State offence and an order that Mr Jones be released after 12 months upon entering into a recognisance in the sum of $500 to be of good behaviour for a period of 12 months for the Commonwealth offence.

Mr Jones appealed against both the State and Commonwealth non-parole periods. He argued that the non-parole periods were manifestly excessive and the judge had given insufficient discount for the State offence when taking into account the guilty plea and other mitigating circumstances.

The sentencing principles were recently reviewed by the Full Court in *R v Riddle* [2012] SASCFC 82. The remarks of The Chief Justice in *R v Padberg* [2010] SASC 189 were adopted. The Chief Justice said:

> It is clear that there is an international market in child pornography, as well as a market within Australia. Those who are part of the market for this material share the responsibility for what is done to the children depicted. The creation and dissemination of child pornography material is a serious social evil, and those who acquire and use such material must be held accountable for the part that they play in the persistence of this social evil ... Offences of this kind will usually require a custodial sentence and will usually call for a period of imprisonment to be served. I mean offences of the kind charged, committed over a significant period of time, involving a substantial amount of pornographic material and involving child pornography of the most serious kind ... It is the objective seriousness of this kind of offending, its prevalence, and the need for deterrence that justify what I have said.

The appeal judge agreed with these statements, noting that this type of offending is serious and has become more prevalent, and that numerous warnings have been given by the Court of Criminal Appeal as to the likely severity of sentences. He quoted the Chief Justice *in R v Padberg* as saying:

> When sentencing offenders, general deterrence must be given a high weighting. The prevalence of child pornography material, and its availability through the internet, mean that potential users of such material must be warned that, if detected, they will be punished most severely.

He concluded that:

1. As discussed in *R v Riddle*, it is difficult to compare head sentences and non-parole periods with other cases involving this type of offending. Each case must be decided on its own facts and the fixing of penalties is not a mathematical exercise. This matter is another example.
2. This case involved a large number of downloads. Mr Jones was not satisfied to only use the material for his own 'short term pleasure' as he described it, but he went a step further and uploaded material to a US-based website which was described by the Australian Federal Police in their summary of facts as follows:

> [The US-based website] ... has been identified as having in excess of forty million users, linking billions of personal photos, graphics, slideshows and video, to hundreds of thousands of websites ... further provides

users with the means to share their personal digital media by email, instant messaging and mobile devices.
3. Children are unable to protect themselves from exploitation. They suffer substantial harm both in the short term and long term and are entitled to be protected by the law and the courts from this prevalent international market of child pornography. They are victims enduring ongoing exploitation and those committing crimes against these defenceless victims must expect to receive severe penalties.
4. As indicated the judge said this case was a serious example of these offences within the range of seriousness coming before the court. I agree with the judge.
5. In my view the judge has not failed to take into account any relevant matter or that he has wrongly taken irrelevant matters into account.
6. In my view, although the discounts given for the pleas of guilty are quite different they are not shown to be in error. Both are within the sentencing judge's broad discretion. Specifically the discount for the State offence was within that discretion.

The appeal was dismissed.

Mr William Pitt

Background to the Case

Mr Pitt had been charged with Sexual Interference [151 CC] under the Canadian Criminal Code, to which he had pled guilty. This Canadian case illustrates some of the difficulties faced when a 'status' offence is presented for a psychological evaluation. In Canada only girls under 12 were absolutely unable to consent to sexual intercourse until 1890, when the age limit was raised to 14. Even then, if the underage girl was married to the party with whom she had sexual intercourse, then it was lawful. In 1988, a new offence called 'sexual interference' prohibited any kind of sexual contact with either boys or girls under the age of 14 irrespective of consent. Also 'sexual exploitation' as an offence was concurrently introduced which made it an offence for an adult to have such contact with boys or girls over 14 but under 18 if there was a relationship of trust or authority with them (e.g., a male high school teacher with a 17-year-old girl). Many suggested and actual nuanced changes to law over the years reflected the complexity of this area (e.g., allowing sex with 'close in age' peers with the window varying from 2 to 5 years depending on the age of child). Similar debates have occurred in other countries (and among states of some countries) often with enforcement not exercised fully depending on the perceived social sensibilities of the particular cases. In May 2008, the age of consent in Canada was lifted to 16 with the intended mission to target sexual predators and pimps using children. However, the number of cases such as William Pitt's have increased.

There was no debate about the facts of the case and no suggestion that William or his 'victim', Rachel, tried to hide their relationship. Neither considered it 'illicit' and it did not draw the attention of their parents. William also had documented history about his medical condition, which was deemed relevant to the courts. The testing administered asked questions about his cognitive capacity and sexual/mental pathology. Risk was a question asked of the examiner. Again, the purpose of the report is to answer questions and provide relevant scientific information to the trier of fact.

In this case, the Crown was asking for significant incarceration for William. The judge was required to impose a mandatory minimum sentence of 2 years. The importance of the sentencing report is that such information often follows the individual to the correctional system where it is used for proper placement (least restrictive environment) and consideration for early release (particularly in non-violent cases). Interesting in this case, a victim impact statement by Rachel identified the community and the law itself as causing her stress (not the relationship with the accused) and lamented the interference with her relationship with William by the authorities.

Relevant in this case is the psychologist's awareness of what other jurisdictions do with similar cases — whether they are common law (like Canada) or not. The impact may not be direct but broadens all participants' perspectives on the relevant issues. The report was deemed useful by all parties in this respect.

Background History

Mr Pitt was born in Montreal and his family moved to Toronto when he was 6 months old. He was adopted at birth. His birth mother was young and drank alcohol to excess during her pregnancy with Mr Pitt. He was diagnosed as suffering Fetal Alcohol Syndrome (FAS) in his early life and has been monitored for most of his life regarding aspects of this disorder. At the age of 17, he met his birth mother and they have had contact several times after that. His adopted father is a manager of an insurance brokerage and his mother works as an elementary school teacher. They reside together in Scarborough. Mr Pitt has a sister who is several years younger than he and who is also adopted. She is 20, is married and moved to Ottawa with her husband where she works at a restaurant. Mr Pitt continues to live with his mother and father.

When asking him about trauma in his life, Mr Pitt described that he was bullied throughout his school years as he was small for his age, quiet and socially withdrawn (all characteristics of FAS). He attended special classes in the public school system and also was at the Melton Home because of his social behaviour. He attended Carrington High School but left before completing their special education program and had to finish his high school diploma with online courses.

After he finished school, Mr Pitt said that he did not do much and then started to look for part-time work. His first job was at a gas bar and he was there for a year. He then worked for a shop changing oil and then was at a furniture warehouse for a month. He also assembled furniture for a year. He most recently was working delivering parcels but was supposed to be there part-time and when he could not change to full time he was dismissed. He is currently applying for work.

He indicated that he likes to cook but he often eats out in fast food restaurants. He drinks alcohol once per week, on weekends, and said that he does not abuse alcohol and does not consider his use problematic. Mr Pitt added that he was a 'pothead' during high school but since then rarely smokes marijuana and has not done so for many months. He said that he does not use other drugs and only used the drug ecstasy on one occasion.

Mr Pitt said that his main joy in life is driving. He has a 2000 Chevy Camaro which he has 'tricked out' and just likes to drive around. He said that he was never attracted to sports very much but does like music and in his spare time will work as a DJ at parties or with his friends.

He has no criminal history.

He described being physically healthy. Mr Pitt said that he has attended many counsellors and continues on with a behaviour therapist now.

Circumstances of the Offence

Mr Pitt was able to describe the nature of the charges to me as sexual assault and sexual interference and he considers these to be of a serious nature. He explained that he met a girl, Rachel, through a friend and she was 15 years old at the time. He was then 22 years old but he explained that all of his friends have always been younger than he as he is able to relate better to that age group. He and Rachel dated for a few weeks — going to the movies and for coffee — and he knew that she was in Grade 9 at the time. However, when Mr Pitt's parents asked her what grade she was in, she told them that she was in Grade 11. Mr Pitt said that Rachel looks a little older than her age but he did discover her age until several weeks after meeting her. He added that he has been to her parents' home and that they knew he was older, for her father had him buy cigarettes for him at the local corner store. During the relationship, Mr Pitt and Rachel had sexual intercourse on two occasions and he wore a condom each time. He added that his mother and teachers in sex education classes made it clear that this was a responsible thing to do and '*drummed it into him*' to act in this way. Mr Pitt and Rachel reportedly mutually agreed to have sexual relations. He said that age was not important to them — what was important were the feelings they had for each other. He said that all other relations after Rachel were with females over 18 years old. However, he indicated that his current girlfriend is about to turn 17. He was unaware at the time of his physical relationship with Rachel that it was legally wrong and neither did the adults in his social scope (including Rachel's parents and his own).

Mr Pitt explained that his girlfriend, Rachel, was concerned about having a sexually transmitted disease from a relationship prior to that with him. They attended a medical clinic together and in the course of that examination she was questioned about Mr Pitt and his age. The clinic contacted the Toronto Police Service who obtained a statement from Rachel and subsequently arrested Mr Pitt.

Assessment

The evaluation of Mr Pitt employed:

- An interview with the offender (5 September 2012)
- Interviews with his parents , George and Fiona Pitt (16 September 2012)
- Cognitive, personality and sexuality testing (6 September 2012)
- Third party records including:
    - Case information — Toronto Police Service
    - Report of Dr Jacob Holmes — 20 October 2000
    - Functional Assessment Report — Dr Janine Orton — 7 December 2000
    - Psychological Evaluation — Trillium Assessment Services — Dr Peter Birkett — 10 September 2004
    - Psychological Assessment — Dr Dusty Adams — 15 March 2006

Tests Administered

- Personality Assessment Inventory (PAI)
- Wechsler Abbreviated Scale of Intelligence – 2 (WASI – 2)
- Color Trails Test
- Wide Range Achievement Test – IV (word reading; sentence comprehension)
- Controlled Oral Word Test (FAS)
- Ruff's 2 and 7 Selective Attention Test
- Brief Visuospatial Memory Test – Revised
- DKefs – 20 Questions Test; Proverbs Test
- Hopkins Verbal Learning Test – Revised
- Test of Memory Malingering (TOMM)

- Sexual Violence Risk – 20 (SVR-20)
- Derogatis Sexual Functioning Inventory (Subtests)
- Behavioral Rating Inventory of Executive Function – Adult (BRIEF-A)
- Clinical Findings.

Mr Pitt presented as a casually dressed male who appeared younger than his stated age. He gave his height as 5 foot 6 inches and weight as 140 pounds. His speech was spontaneous revealing below average vocabulary and syntax although he did not appear to have any difficulties comprehending questions. His affect fluctuated appropriately to the topics of discussion.

Mr Pitt has undergone numerous psychological assessments over the years. A Paediatric Consultant (Dr Jacob Holmes) wrote in 1999 that 'Bill is a 12-year-old boy who has been diagnosed with Fetal Alcohol Syndrome, Attention Deficit Disorder, Oppositional Defiant Disorder and who has severe behaviour problems' and he urged funding for special education to assist Mr Pitt. Chronologically, the first formal psychological report I have reviewed is from Dr Jane Orton (when Mr Pitt was 13 years old). She found that Mr Pitt presented with overall intellectual ability at the 18th percentile with weaker abilities in the verbal domain. She said that 'his profile was commensurate with the cognitive deficits typically identified in one of the Fetal Alcohol Spectrum Disorders and he also had a significant learning disability in arithmetic'. She states regarding his behaviour he 'is prone to impulsive, poorly thought-out decisions that alienate others'. He apparently had 'marked deficits in memory, a rather immature social style and a rigid and highly reactive personality'. She goes on to say that 'Bill is at considerable risk of being manipulated by others since he does not consider others' motives and, without the constant supervision and vigilance of his family could easily be persuaded to engage in inappropriate activities'.

In Grade 11, when he was 17 years, he underwent another formal psychological evaluation. The report by Dr Peter Birkett indicated that he found 'significant deficits occurred in the area of adaptive living skills. Compounding these are high levels of personal maladjustment'. Although Mr Pitt was found to have reasonable core academic skills, it was cautioned — 'this does not necessarily indicate that Billy is capable of skilfully applying these cognitive abilities in daily living contexts; factors such as poor judgement, anxiety, impulsivity and inconsistent task motivation could negatively impact his performance'.

At the age of 19, Mr Pitt was evaluated by another psychologist — Dr Deanna Adams. She found that he had deficits typical of Fetal Alcohol Spectrum Disorder such as slow information processing speed, poor organisational abilities, poor emotional regulation, fatigue and poor stamina and lower verbal skills. She concluded that

> Bill is a young man who is clearly struggling as he transitions to adulthood. His current level of functioning is primarily maintained through the ongoing and consistent support provided by his parents. Even with this level of support, he has been unable to maintain a level of employment that could sustain his independence over the long term and his struggle can be directly attributable to the effects of his disability. Without the support that he receives, Bill would be at an extreme risk for the challenges faced by many young people with FASD (including chronic unemployment, poor mental and physical health, poverty, possible homelessness etc.).

We also conducted a brief review of some major cognitive functions with Mr Pitt. Cognitive testing is only valid if sufficient effort has been applied to the tasks. To this end, we administered the TOMM — a recognition memory test which appears difficult but which is relatively easy, even for genuinely compromised patients. Fifty line drawings of common objects are shown to the patient and then he or she is to distinguish ones they had been shown from other line drawings that had never been shown in a binary display. Mr Pitt showed good performance with scores of (49/50 and 50/50) on the two trials and a perfect score as well on a retention trial. With this finding, I am able to present his testing scores with confidence as representing a valid cognitive profile.

We gave Mr Pitt the WASI-2, a current abbreviation of the Wechsler intelligence tests. His full scale IQ was in the low average range with a statistically significant advantage on the non-verbal tests, as was found in previous evaluations.

Mr Pitt's academic skills were measured with the Wide Range Achievement Test. His word reading was at the 58th percentile (Grade 12.7) and his sentence comprehension was at the 77th percentile (greater that Grade 12.9 the ceiling for this test).

Mr Pitt's attentional abilities were measured with the 2 & 7 test, which requires the patient to cancel these two digits from a mixed display over a period of five minutes. The target numbers are buried in lists of either letters (which makes detection easy) or other numbers, which is considerably harder. Compared to his age peers, on the easy task his performance was below average in the time he took to complete but was moderately impaired in accuracy of detection. On the more difficult task, Mr Pitt was moderately impaired in speed of performance and again mildly to moderately impaired in his accuracy on this measure of selective attention.

We measured Mr Pitt's memory abilities using a variety of materials. His ability to learn and recall a list of 12 words over three trials was moderately impaired (overall recall at the only the 1st percentile). He was able to recognise the words read to him from a mixed group of words some of which had not been read to him. We administered a parallel task, which, instead of words, asks the patient to learn and recall over three trials a display of six unusual geometric shapes. His abilities here were significantly better than with words and he scored in the low average range on all trials and on a delayed recall. His recognition of the shapes later was without error.

We gave Mr Pitt several executive functioning tests, requiring more complex reasoning. On Coloured Trails, which require the patient to quickly connect a series of circles in sequence, Mr Pitt scored in the average range. However, on verbal fluency (the ability to generate words beginning with a target letter on demand) he was very impaired. He was able to solve a test that required the patient to ask questions of the examiner to find a solution. He had some struggles in explaining common proverbs but was able overall to achieve a satisfactory score.

Mr Pitt and his mother completed the Behavior Rating Inventory of Executive Functions — Adult — which is both a self-rating and observer-rating questionnaire that captures patients' views of their own executive functions or self-regulation in their everyday environment. Such functions include ability to initiate behaviours, inhibit competing actions, select relevant goals, plan and organise a means to solve complex problems, shift problem solving strategies flexibly, regulate emotions and monitor and evaluate behaviour. For Mr Pitt all three validity scales were within acceptable limits. On this measure Mr Pitt several of his self-ratings were above the clinical threshold of an 'abnormal' finding. For example, his rating of his lack of ability to inhibit his actions was at the 95th percentile and this was also seen on his ability to switch or change focus in his problems solving skills. He also breached the statistical threshold on the scale which gauges an individual's ability to keep track of their own behaviour and effects on others. He also indicated some difficulty with working memory — the capacity to actively hold information in mind for the purpose of completing a task or working on a separate problem. Overall the test indicates that his difficulties in executive functions are all above the norm but not dramatically elevated. His mother's rating (also valid) was similar in pointing out lack of inhibitory behaviours, in particular.

I had Mr Pitt complete the Personality Assessment Inventory (PAI) to survey his mental health functioning. This modern instrument contains multiple validity indices to gauge the test-takers' cooperation. The analysis of the main validity scales revealed 'slight' distortion which is the lowest rating possible and I thus present the computerised interpretation of his profile, keeping in mind that this narrative is best thought of as suggested hypotheses since it is based on group norms:

The PAI clinical profile reveals no marked elevations that should be considered to indicate the presence of clinical psychopathology. Scores on one or more scales do, however, show moderate elevations that may reflect sources of difficulty for the person. These potential problem areas are described below.

He reports a personality style that involves a degree of adventurousness, risk-taking, and a tendency to be rather impulsive. Others may view him as pragmatic and perhaps unsympathetic in his relationships. His responses suggest that he has a history of antisocial behaviour and may have manifested a conduct disorder during adolescence. He may have been involved in illegal occupations or engaged in criminal acts involving theft, destruction of property, or physical aggression toward others.

It appears that the respondent is quite impulsive and prone to behaviours likely to be self-harmful or self-destructive (such as those involving spending, sex, and/or substance abuse) with little forethought as to the potential consequences of these behaviours.

Certain elements of the respondent's self-description suggest that others are likely to see him as being withdrawn, aloof, and somewhat unconventional.

The respondent describes himself as being more wary and sensitive in interpersonal relationships than the average adult. Others are likely to see him as tough-minded, sceptical, and somewhat hostile.

According to the respondent's self-report, he describes NO significant problems in the following areas: problems with empathy; unhappiness and depression; unusually elevated mood or heightened activity; marked anxiety; problematic behaviours used to manage anxiety; difficulties with health or physical functioning. Also, he reports NO significant problems with alcohol or drug abuse or dependence. However, attention should be paid to the possibility of denial of problems with drinking or drug use, as the respondent described certain personality characteristics that are often associated with involvement with alcohol or drugs.

The self-concept of the respondent appears to involve a self-evaluation that has both positive and negative aspects. His attitudes about himself may vary from states of pessimism and self-doubt to periods of relative self-confidence and self-satisfaction. Some fluctuation in self-esteem may be observed as a function of his current circumstances, although these fluctuations will not be extreme and are comparable to those experienced by most adults. During stressful times in particular, he is prone to be somewhat self-critical, uncertain, and indecisive.

The respondent's interpersonal style seems best characterised as being very uncomfortable in social situations. He appears to have little interest in or need for interacting with others and likely takes a rather passive, submissive stance when dealing with others. This lack of interest and initiative may result in his being socially isolated, avoiding most social interactions rather than run the risk of being forced to make an active commitment to a relationship.

In considering the social environment of the respondent with respect to perceived stressors and the availability of social supports with which to deal with these stressors, his responses indicate that both his recent level of stress and his perceived level of social support are about average in comparison to normal adults. The reasonably low stress environment and the intact social support system are both favorable prognostic signs for future adjustment.

Because of the nature of the charges Mr Pitt faces, I attempted to understand key elements of his sexuality using some subscales from the Derogatis Sexual Functioning Inventory. He presents with average knowledge of human sexual functioning and hygiene, describes an average level of sexual drive, has a typical range of sexual experiences and described a low average range of sexual fantasy. His attitudes towards sexual matters falls in the average range (between conservative and liberal). Research has shown that sexual offenders frequently have very deviant profiles on the DSFI. Mr Pitt's psychosexual profile is generally consistent with the norm for heterosexual males. I reviewed a range of paraphilias from DSM-IV TR (sexual behaviours that causes distress to the individual or harm to others) and he indicated that he does not engage in any of these and was indeed puzzled that anyone would participate in these acts.

You have also asked me to provide a risk evaluation on Mr Pitt. The standard for non-incarcerated individuals is referred to as a structured professional judgement typically based on review of a set number of issues empirically related to a target behaviour occurring. For Mr Pitt, I used the Sexual Violence Risk–20 which is a checklist of 20 risk factors all shown to predict or relate to sexual violence. There is no evidence that he has suffered from a psychopathic personality disorder or suffered any form of major mental illness (such as psychosis or mania) but he has some measured cognitive deficits. He has no significant substance use problems. He does not show suicidal or homicidal ideation. He has little problem in establishing relationships but they are always with persons younger than he. He has no past non-sexual violent offences. There is no record of past supervision failures. He does not have 'high density' sex offences recorded — that is, a high number of sexual offences occurring in a short period of time when at risk to do so. There is no record of multiple sex offence types – sexual offences that vary in terms of nature and victim type (e.g., voyeurism, exhibitionism, rape) with various degrees of coercion and victims that range from children through adolescents to adults and the elderly and different genders or acquaintanceship. There is no record of escalation in frequency or severity of offences. He has no past acts of sexual violence. He holds no personal attitudes or beliefs that would support or condone sexual violence against others and he indicated that sexual activities with children are wrong. The SVR-20 rating does not reveal any elevation in risk above the general population and therefore Mr Pitt would be classified as 'low risk' to commit a future sex offence.

Opinion

Mr William Pitt is a 24-year-old male charged with having sexual contact with a female who was 15 years old at the time (when he was 22). He has been diagnosed since childhood with Fetal Alcohol Syndrome (FAS) and while he shows generally average overall cognitive functioning has pockets of cognitive difficulties including attention and some executive reasoning. As noted by previous assessors, such difficulties are common in this clinical population.

Fetal Alcohol Syndrome and its associated difficulties have been recognised for over forty years. The behavioural difficulties specific to FAS are thought directly linked to abnormalities of brain development in utero. Recent reviews of outcome of FAS found that over 50% of patients over the age of 20 had engaged in 'Inappropriate Sexual Behaviours' (see Streissguth et al., 2004). Indeed, it is the most frequent adverse life outcome in this population and is linked to problems in acquiring adaptive behavioural functioning and is not directly linked with functioning tapped in routine IQ tests (only 24% of individuals with FAS have IQ's below 70).

The nexus between FAS and legal 'offending behaviour' is necessary to consider in weighing appropriate penalties. This has been comprehensively and articulately reviewed by several members of the Faculty of Law at the University of Ottawa (see Chartrand & Forbes-Chilibeck, 2003). He argues that traditional sentencing principles are inappropriate and calls for an approach that is sensitive to the unique circumstances of offenders with FAS. Often the offending behaviour is thought to arise from impulsive behaviour and brain functions involving judgement and reasoning and the inability or impairment in understanding cause and effect. In Mr Pitt's case, his offending was ultimately caused by association with younger persons who are of similar social maturity to himself rather than his age peers. Interestingly, in Finland although the age of consent for sexual behaviour is also 16, a contact with an adult and a person under the age of 16 may not be deemed to be unlawful if 'there is no great difference in the ages or the mental and physical maturity of the persons involved' (see section 6, subsection 2 Criminal Code of Finland; Ministry of Justice [2009]). Although Mr Pitt's offence rests on the status of his sexual partner it nonetheless leaves him as a 'sexual offender' with all the concomitant social residual from that categorisation.

A secondary concern relates to the penalty of incarceration for Mr Pitt. Due to his FAS, he has been repeatedly identified by professionals as a vulnerable individual prone to being manipulated or abused by others. He remains unable to live completely independent at this point in his life and this reflects his difficulties in planning, self-monitoring and management of his behaviour. In some respects, his long-term association with younger persons rather than age peers has protected him from the exploitation or frank abuse that individuals with FAS often endure from other adults. This would not be the case in any adult prison or jail. I also am of the opinion that incarceration would not serve the goal of protection of society.

Using structured professional guidelines, Mr Pitt also presents as a low risk for future sexual violence (there is no category of 'no risk'). There is no evidence of his use of violence with his sexual behaviour and his father and mother described him as a gentle, caring and loyal young man who was never looking for casual sex but a stable long-term heterosexual relationship. It was this that he was seeking with his underage girlfriend. Mr Pitt is now aware of the concrete need for him to seek relationships with females over the legal age of consent.

Mr Leonard Panther

Background to the Case

This is another interesting Australian case that examines the crime of 'Unlawful Sexual Intercourse' and demonstrates how the law may sometime be flexible to reflect justice. This was a landmark case. Mr Panther was referred by his solicitor for a psychological assessment for matters relevant to sentencing.

Background History

Family

Mr Panther was born in the township of Bintu, Southern Sudan, on 8 November 1982 and is now aged 30 years. He said he came from a large family that comprised 10 children. Mr Panther indicated that he left Sudan at age 16 years, first travelling to Kenya, before being accepted as a refugee, and then being sponsored by his cousin to come to Australia, arriving on 4 July 2002.

Mr Panther indicated that his parents were both deceased. He said his mother died in 1995, and that he witnessed her being murdered by Northern Sudanese government soldiers, when she was shot multiple times in the stomach. He said that at the time his mother was 8 months pregnant with her 11th child. Mr Panther indicated that his memory of his mother's death, though only aged 11 years, was very powerful. He said her death followed him being attacked by soldiers, who bayoneted him in the leg. He said his mother, while protesting their violence, was shot. Mr Panther said the image of the 8-month foetus 'exploding' from his mother's stomach remained vivid in his mind.

Mr Panther indicated that his mother died aged in her thirties, having married at age 15 years. He said that marrying young was a part of the Sudanese culture. Mr Panther described his mother as having been '*a very loving person*' and that he felt a great deal of pain over her loss. He said he also felt much guilt for not being able to prevent the murder.

Mr Panther stated that his father died in 2007, aged in his sixties, from cancer. Mr Panther said that at the time his father was living in Sudan, and he described him as '*a good man*'. He said he last saw his father in 1998, and indicated that, as his father's eldest son, their relationship was particularly close. Mr Panther said he was badly affected when he learnt of his father's death. He said that at the time he received the news from his brother via a telephone call, while driving his vehicle. He said he crashed the car, but was not badly injured. He said was unable to drive because of the emotional distress he experienced at the time.

Mr Panther indicated that his childhood memories were fraught with tragedy and loss. He indicated that he had had nine siblings: eight sisters and one brother — but now only three siblings (two sisters and a brother) alive and living in South Sudan.

Mr Panther said that in 1991, he witnessed the family's home being bombed. Inside the home six of his sisters were all killed. Mr Panther said that at the time he had been playing outside. Mr Panther stated that his two surviving sisters, Nina and Noonah were now aged 26 and 25 years respectively. He said he last spoke with them on 26 December 2013, and that at the time they were concerned for their safety as more political fighting was taking place.

Mr Panther indicated that he had one brother Kume, who is now aged 23 years, who lived within the United Nations section of South Sudan. Mr Panther indicated that he had spoken with his brother the day previous, and was told that his brother was also uncertain about his future. Mr Panther indicated that people died all the time in his homeland.

Mr Panther indicated that he was currently single, but had previously been involved in two significant relationships. He said the first of those relationships was with partner Martha (1996–2001). Mr Panther described the relationship as '*wonderful and happy*' and that he was a few years older than his first partner, who was '*a wonderful person*'. Mr Panther said that at the time they were living in South Sudan. Mr Panther said the relationship ended because of the civil war, where the township where he was living was destroyed, and he was removed. Mr Panther said he was very distressed by the relationship ending, and indicated that they had a child together, a 13-year-old son, Picka, who was now living in Australia. Mr Panther said he had been the primary carer of his son between 2008 and 2012 and described him as '*a lovely boy*'. He said his son was now living with his female cousin in Melbourne.

Mr Panther said he had successfully applied to get his son to Australia in 2008. He said they travelled to South Sudan for a brief trip (19 May 2013–3 June 2013), but on his return he thought it was best for his son to live with his female cousin (the child's aunt) in Melbourne, until his criminal matters were resolved and he could join them in Melbourne.

Mr Panther said his second significant partner was Nua (2011–2013), who was of Sudanese background but from a different tribal clan. He said that the relationship was '*good*', but he perceived he was never accepted by her parents. Mr Panther indicated that she was about 10 years younger than he. Mr Panther said that he believed her parents prejudice against him was largely due to their tribal-clan differences, and the fact that he did not have living parents. Mr Panther indicated that during their relationship she became pregnant on three occasions, but her parents were opposed to their daughter having a child with him and he believed the pressure they put on her, forced her to have the pregnancies terminated.

At the time of her third pregnancy in June 2013, Mr Panther said he threatened to leave the relationship if she did not have their child. He said that against his wishes she chose to have an abortion, and so he left the relationship and they ceased talking. Mr Panther said that two weeks later (26 June 2013) police arrived at his house and he was charged with his current offences.

Mr Panther indicated that he currently lived in student accommodation in Adelaide in a two-bedroom unit. He said he was living there by himself, and had been there since 2013. He said he was happy there, but struggled to meet the rental payments, because his state welfare payments had been stopped.

Education

Mr Panther stated that he completed approximately six years of education while living in Sudan and perceived that their education system was reasonable, and that he enjoyed his time at school. He said he had many friends, and was an '*above-average*' student. Mr Panther indicated that his favourite subjects were Religion and Science, while his least favourite subject was Mathematics. He said that his schooling in Sudan finished when he left the country in 1998. He said he travelled from South Sudan to Makal, then to Esski in Kenya (1998–2000); and then to Australia (July 2002). He said that in the refugee camp in Kenya, he sat his Year 7 exams.

Mr Panther indicated that in 2002 he studied English for six months, then underwent distance learning. Mr Panther stated that he subsequently completed successfully a foundation course for entrance to university and then attended Diskin University (2009) where he commenced studying an Arts degree. He said he continued that course through to 2012, but found it difficult to focus on his studies due to external factors. He said that in 2013 he changed his course to study a Bachelor of Health Science, but that he had failed two first-year subjects. Mr Panther said that he planned, in 2014, to move interstate where he had been accepted to study at Lacross University for a degree of Health Sciences. He said it was a four-year Bachelor Degree that was due to start in March 2014.

Vocational History

Mr Panther said that since coming to Australia he had been studying, and had not found employment. He said that at the time of the assessment he had also been without any income source, because he had been excluded from his welfare allowance.

Health

Mr Panther indicated that his physical health was *'excellent'*. He said he sustained a major stabbing injury to his leg, when in 1995 when he was stabbed with a bayonet by military soldiers attacking his village. He said that at the same time his mother was killed, and died trying to protect him. Mr Panther indicated that when he was aged 10 years he had sustained some head injuries from falling into a well. In more recent times, Mr Panther said he had had an operation on his right hand (July 2013) through the Royal Mulberry Hospital, and that the outcome was successful. More recently he said he was assaulted by someone with a stick and knocked unconscious. He said it was a case of 'wrong identity'. Mr Panther rated his current physical health at 10/10. He said that the best his physical health had been was 10/10, the worst 2/10.

Mental Health

Mr Panther indicated that his mental health was *'good'*. Mr Panther indicated that currently his main stresses were court, and his siblings problems in Sudan, where he feared for their lives. Mr Panther indicated that he was not aware of being diagnosed in the past with any mental health problems, or ever been treated for any. He denied being depressed and said that his mood was stable. He denied having problems with anger. Mr Panther said that in the past he had been a victim of physical abuse, when he was attacked by soldiers. He said he had never really been a victim of emotional or sexual abuse. Mr Panther rated his current mental health at 10/10. He said that the best his mental health had been was 10/10, the worst 1/10.

Substance Use

Mr Panther denied using alcohol, cannabis, methamphetamine, ecstasy, hallucinogenic drugs (e.g., LSD), heroin, cocaine, morphine and prescription medication.

Gambling Issues

Mr Panther indicated that he did not have a gambling problem.

Past Criminal History

Mr Jones indicated that he had no prior history of offending.

Current Criminal Charges

It is indicated that Mr Panther is facing charges of Unlawful Sexual Intercourse (Offence date: between August 2011 and 30 August 2011). Mr Panther said he had had a loving relationship with partner (2011–2013) for which in evidence he had many photographs of them in a romantic context. He indicated that his partner was about 10 years younger than he. Mr Panther said they were both of Sudanese background, but were from different tribal clans. He said he perceived he was never accepted by her parents, who were prejudiced against him because of their tribal-clan differences, and the fact that he did not have living parents.

Mr Panther indicated that during their relationship Nua became pregnant to him on three occasions, but her parents were opposed to their daughter having a child with him. He believed the parents pressured her to have the pregnancies terminated. At the time of her third pregnancy in June 2013, Nua said he threatened to leave the relationship if she did not have their child. He said that against his wishes she chose to have an abortion, and so he left the relationship and they ceased talking. Mr Panther said that about two weeks later police arrived at his house and he was charged with his current offence. It was noted that Sudanese culture allows consensual sexual behaviour between consenting partners as young as 10 years old (or age of the onset of puberty).

Rehabilitation History

Mr Panther stated that he had not participated in any previous rehabilitation, but was willing to undertake any programs recommended by the court.

Assessment

Behaviour During Assessment

At the commencement of the assessment, the nature and purpose of the assessment was explained to Mr Panther in order that a psychological report could be prepared for the court. The limitations of confidentiality in this context were explained.

Mr Panther presented as a 29 year-old Sudanese male of above average height and thin build. Mr Panther was clean-shaven, with a dark complexion and short, neatly groomed, dark hair. He wore a pink and white business shirt, dark grey waistcoat and dark trousers. He did not wear any jewelry nor did he have visible tattoos or piercings on his person. Mr Panther was polite and cooperative throughout the assessment and did not appear to have any difficulty understanding the questions asked. The assessment took place at Black and Associates Psychologists' offices on 4 January 2014, between 2.00 pm and 4.30 pm.

Cognitive Functioning

The Complex Figure Test was administered in order to assess Mr Panther's ability to organise and plan visual spatial information. This test also provides an indication of the person's higher order processing. Savage et al. (1999) determined a scoring system, which examines the person's strategy sophistication in reproducing the principal components of the figure, and generates a score (maximum = 6) from this, that measures the level of strategy sophistication associated with the person's copy. This measure may be sensitive to brain impairment.

Mr Panther's strategy score indicated that the strategy adopted was logical and effective and did not suggest that there was any frontal lobe impairment.

The Kaufman Brief Intelligence Test (K-BIT) is a well-developed psychological test that provides an indication of both a person's verbal, non-verbal intelligence, and overall measure of 'global intelligence'. The instrument is well standardised, based on extensive sampling in the United States and Australia, and has been adapted for an Australian population.

The K-BIT was administered and indicated that Mr Panther was in the average ($90 < IQ < 110$) range of intelligence and around the 30th percentile of the age equivalent population. Mr Panther's verbal IQ was around the 34th percentile while his non-verbal IQ was around the 30th percentile. This did not show a significant difference between his verbal and nonverbal abilities.

Personality Profile

The revised NEO Personality Inventory (Form S) was used to measure Mr Panther's personality using a dimensional approach. The instrument is a standardised self-report measure, which allows the clinician to measure personality traits that characterise the individual and provide information, which can assist the assessment of likely responsiveness to treatment and prognosis prediction.

Mr Panther's 'personality' profile indicated that he is within the *average* range for the 'Extraversion' (E), 'Openness' (O), 'Agreeableness' (A) and 'Conscientiousness' (C) factor scores; and within the *low* range for the 'Neuroticism' (N) factor score.

Such a personality profile indicated that Mr Panther is emotionally stable and able to deal effectively with 'Stress'. He is a person who was very warm and friendly towards others and enjoyed the company of people in most social situations. Mr Panther, at times, is guarded about his feelings, but open about his values. He had limited trust in other people but is very compliant and willing to cooperate with others. He is extremely tender minded. Mr Jones sees himself as very dutiful, disciplined and deliberate and able to follow tasks through to their completion.

Clinical Profile

The Personality Assessment Inventory (PAI) was used to objectively assess aspects of Mr Panther's clinical profile. The PAI is a standardised self-report questionnaire that provides a profile of a person based on his or her responses to items that examine aspects of a person's behaviour and thinking. The measure includes four primary sets of scales: validity scales, clinical scales, treatment scales, and interpersonal scales. The instrument has been normed with a Census–matched Standardisation sample ($N = 1,000$), College Sample ($N = 1,051$), Clinical sample ($N = 1,246$) and Public Safety Sample group ($N = 17,757$).

It was indicated that Mr Panther's responses were generally consistent, and did not show an overly positive or overly negative response set to the questions. Mr Panther's PAI 'clinical' profile indicated he was elevated on measures of Somatisation, Physiological–Anxiety, Traumatic Stress, Affective–Depression, Hypervigilance and Negative Relationships. Such a configuration of clinical scales suggested that Mr Panther is a person with significant tension, unhappiness and pessimism. Although Mr Panther was quite distressed and acutely aware of his need for help, his low energy level, tension, and withdrawal makes it difficult for him to engage in treatment. Various stressors, both past and present, have adversely affected his self-esteem, and he views himself as ineffectual and powerless to change his life direction. These disruptions have left him feeling uncertain about goals and priorities, and tense and pessimistic about what the future may hold. He is likely to have difficulties concentrating and in making decisions, and the combination of hopelessness, anxiety, and stress apparent in his scores placed him at increased risk of self-harm.

Mr Panther's PAI treatment profile was significantly elevated on measures of 'Stress' and 'Non-Support'. The treatment profile indicated that Mr Panther is very passive in his nature, but experiences significant levels of

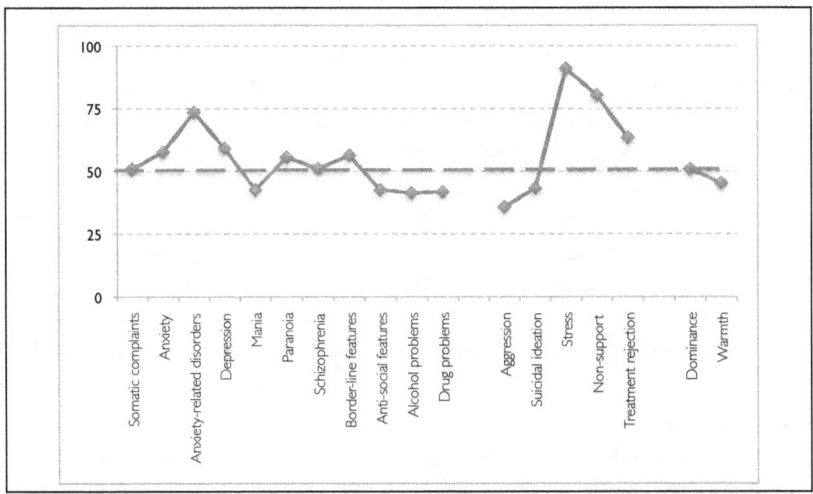

Figure 3.3 Mr Panther's clinical profile (compared with the community normative data [T = 50]).

stress in his life. It was also indicated that he tends to have very limited support from family and friends. On the interpersonal scales (i.e., the way that a person relates to others), Mr Panther was average on the 'Dominance' scale and average on the 'Warmth' scale. Mr Panther's interpersonal style is best characterised as one of autonomy and balance. He has the capacity to adapt to a wide range of interpersonal situations, where he is able to both lead and follow, and able to balance practicality and sentiment. Mr Panther's assertiveness, friendliness and concern for others were typical of that shown by most 'normal' adults.

Opinion

What Was Mr Panther's Psychological Status?

Mr Panther was raised in war-torn South Sudan, and as a child was subjected to horrendous trauma. Among such trauma he witnessed the death of his mother, who was violently shot while 8 months pregnant, and the deaths of his sisters who were killed when the family home was bombed and they were inside, while Mr Panther was playing outside. Ultimately Mr Panther fled Sudan as a consequence of the civil war, and at age 17 years came to Australia as a sponsored refugee. It was indicated that at the time he left behind him his then partner and one-year-old child. Mr Panther indicated that in 2008, he managed to have his son come to live with him in Australia, and indicated that his son had remained in Australia since that time, and was now living with his aunt while Mr Panther's legal matters were being resolved.

Mr Panther said that since coming to Australia his focus had been largely on education where he initially completed studies in English, before successfully completing a tertiary entrance program. He said he had struggled with his university studies since 2009, and most recently had commenced a Health Science degree. He said in 2014 he hoped to continue studying health science interstate.

It was indicated that in 2011 Mr Panther began a relationship with partner, Nua, a Sudanese female 10 years younger than he. It is noted that in Sudan relationships and marriage were legally sanctioned between consenting partners from as young as 10 years of age (or from the age of puberty).

Mr Panther indicated that his general physical health was good, but that he had been previously a victim of a stabbing, when soldiers bayoneted his leg at the same time that his mother was killed. He did not report having any significant mental health problems, and indicated he had never drunk alcohol nor consumed illicit drugs. He reported no history of gambling and no history of criminal offending behaviour.

The preliminary neuropsychological screening suggested that there was no evidence of executive planning dysfunction. The intellectual assessment indicated that Mr Panther was in the average ($90 < IQ < 110$) range of intelligence and around the 30th percentile of the age equivalent population.

Mr Panther's personality profile indicated that he was within the *average* range for the 'Extraversion' (E), 'Openness' (O), 'Agreeableness' (A) and 'Conscientiousness' (C) factor scores; and within the *low* range for the 'Neuroticism' (N) factor score. Such a personality profile indicates that Mr Panther is emotionally stable and able to deal effectively with stress. He is a person who is very warm and friendly towards others and enjoys the company of people in most social situations. Mr Panther, at times, was guarded about his feelings, but was open about his values. He has limited trust in other people but was very compliant and willing to cooperate with others. He was extremely tender minded. Mr Panther sees himself as very dutiful, disciplined and deliberate and able to follow tasks through to their completion.

Mr Panther's PAI clinical profile indicates he is elevated on measures of Somatisation, Physiological-Anxiety, Traumatic Stress, Affective-Depression, Hypervigilance and Negative Relationships. Mr Panther's PAI treatment profile was significantly elevated on measures of stress and nonsupport. The treatment profile indicates that Mr Panther is very passive in nature, but experiences significant levels of stress in his life. It was also indicated he has very limited support from family and friends. On the interpersonal scales (i.e., the way that a person relates to others) Mr Panther was average on the dominance scale and average on the warmth scale. His interpersonal style is best characterised as one of autonomy and balance. Mr

Panther has the capacity to adapt to a wide range of interpersonal situations, where he is able to both lead and follow, and able to balance practicality and sentiment. Mr Panther's assertiveness, friendliness and concern for others were typical of that shown by most 'normal' adults.

Based on data from Mr Panther's background history and the psychological testing, a range of DSM-5 diagnostic hypotheses can be advanced that include:

- Posttraumatic Stress Disorder (refer DSM-5, pp. 271-280))
- Adjustment Disorder With Mixed Anxiety and Depressed Mood (refer DSM-5, pp. 286-289).

What Is the Relationship Between Mr Panther's Psychological Condition and the Offending?

It is indicated that Mr Panther is facing charges of Unlawful Sexual Intercourse (offence dates: between August 2011 and 30 August 2011). Mr Panther said he had a loving and affectionate relationship with his partner (2011–2013) for which in evidence he had many photographs of them in a romantic context. He indicated that his partner was about 10 years younger than he. Mr Panther said they were both of Sudanese background, but were from different tribal clans. He said he perceived he was never accepted by her parents who were prejudiced against him because of their tribal-clan differences, and the fact that he did not have living parents.

Mr Panther indicated that during their relationship his partner became pregnant to him on three occasions, but her parents were opposed to their daughter having a child with him. He believed the parents pressured her to have the pregnancies terminated. At the time of her third pregnancy in June 2013, Mr Panther said he threatened to leave the relationship if she did not have their child. He said that against his wishes she chose to have an abortion, and so he left the relationship and they ceased talking. Mr Panther said that about two weeks later police arrived at his house and he was charged with his current offence.

It is noted that Sudanese culture allowed consensual sexual behaviour between consenting partners as young as 10 years old (or age of the onset of puberty).

Mr Panther's psychological profile indicated that he had significant clinical symptoms related to his past trauma that had remained unresolved. He had essentially lost most of his family through trauma, and for him, life revolved around family and children. Mr Panther's relationship with a younger woman was consistent with cultural norms when he established his relationship, and that there did not appear to be any problems until Mr Panther terminated their relationship because of her reluctance to continue her pregnancy. Mr Panther did not deny having a sexual relationship with his partner, but indicated it was consensual and consistent with their cultural norms, where younger women were often involved with older men.

Given the enormous traumas and life-threatening scenarios Mr Panther has endured, it is ironic that he is at risk of incarceration, after being given Australian refugee status — for maintaining Sudanese cultural behaviour, which has brought him into conflict with Australian law.

What Rehabilitation Is Recommended to Reduce Mr Panther's Risk of Re-Offending?

The assessment indicated Mr Panther has psychological problems in areas of Complex Post-Traumatic Stress, Anxiety, and Depression. It is therefore recommended that Mr Panther be referred to an appropriate mental health professional (psychologist/psychiatrist) to address these mental health issues.

Court Outcome

The judge's sentencing remarks were as follows:

> Mr Panther, you have pleaded guilty to a charge of unlawful sexual intercourse. The circumstances of this offending are, at least in my experience, unique. I will set out what I understand to be the factual basis. You are 29. The complainant's date of birth is not entirely clear, but it has been agreed between the prosecution and the defence that her date of birth is accepted to be 11 February 1995. On that basis, she is now 19. You both come from Sudan. You arrived as a refugee, albeit sponsored by a relative, in July 2002. The complainant arrived quite independently with her parents and three younger brothers in 2002, or at least that is when the family arrived.
>
> I mention briefly, by way of background, that you had apparently been in a sexual relationship with a woman in Sudan between 1996 and 2001 when you were aged between 12 and 17. Your partner was younger than you. A son was born of that relationship when you were 16. He is now 13 and was living with you. He is presently living with a relative interstate until these proceedings are concluded.
>
> Apparently the age of consent in Sudan is, for girls at least, 10, or at the onset of puberty. Your counsel says that when you came to Australia, the only advice you received about sexual mores was AIDS advice. You did not know that the age of consent was 17. That is, of course, no excuse.
>
> These proceedings came to be started in about July last year. The complainant was then 18. She was still going to school. She went to a school counsellor and said she was pregnant as a result of being raped. She went on to allege that she had been raped by you since she was 12. The matter was then immediately reported to the police. She gave two statements to that effect. You were charged with unlawful sexual intercourse and rape.

After your lawyers provided materials to the prosecution, it became apparent to the prosecution that they could not rely on the girl's statements. It is agreed between the prosecution and the defence that you and the complainant were engaged in a sexual relationship in 2011 when the complainant was 16. That relationship continued past the complainant's 17th birthday, and concluded some 18 months later in June 2013. During the course of the relationship, the complainant had three pregnancies terminated. The first was in October 2011 when she was 16, the second in October 2012 when she was 17, and the third in June 2013 when she was 18.

Submissions were put on your behalf by your counsel, and in the psychological report dated 3 February 2014. It seems that you and the complainant come from different tribal groups in Sudan. The complainant's parents did not approve of you, partly because of the tribal difference, but also because both of your parents are dead. Apparently that makes you less acceptable as a partner for their daughter. Although you went along to the appointments with the doctor the times the complainant had the first two abortions, you did not want her to have the abortions. You believed that her parents pressured her into having them because they disapproved of you. The complainant was given counselling and contraception advice after the first termination. You told the complainant that if she went ahead with the third termination in June 2013, you would terminate the relationship. When she said she was going ahead with it, you left. Subsequently she made the complaints which led to the police involvement.

As I say, the prosecution does not rely on her two witness statements. The prosecution does not allege that you had a sexual relationship with her since she was 12. You are to be sentenced on the basis that it occurred when she was 16. It is not alleged the relationship was non-consensual; it is agreed that it was. You have had to face a rape charge which has now been withdrawn. The consensual relationship finished in June 2013. You broke it off when the complainant said she was going ahead with the third termination. You pleaded guilty in the Magistrates Court, although a fresh information was laid in this court. The Crown tenders no victim impact statement.

I turn to your background. You are 29 and have no prior court appearances of any sort. You were born in Sudan, the eldest of 10 children. You saw first-hand the violence of the civil war. Your mother, who was then pregnant, was killed in front of you. At the same time, you were bayoneted by solders. Some of your siblings were killed. You were 11 at the time. You fled Sudan as a refugee to other parts of Africa and then came to Australia as a refugee in 2002. You had the care of your son when he came to Australia in 2008, and that remained the case until 2012 when he was sent to the care of a relative.

Although you had limited schooling in Africa, you have undertaken bridging courses to prepare you for university studies. You attended university in 2009 when you commenced an Arts Degree but you discontinued that in 2012 because you were having difficulty focusing on your studies. You changed your course in 2013 to a Bachelor of Health Science course, but failed some of the subjects in first year. You plan in March this year to move to another university.

Ordinarily the court would impose a sentence of imprisonment for a charge of unlawful sexual intercourse. That is so because minors are to be protected from their vulnerability and immaturity. That is particularly so where older perpetrators are involved. When the sexual relationship began, the complainant was 16 and you were 26. It is a primary policy of the criminal law to protect children from sexual predators.

For any offence involving the sexual exploitation of a child, a paramount consideration is given to the need for deterrence. However, in my view, the facts of this case are so unusual that questions of general and personal deterrence do not have the significance that they usually do have. The courts have recognised that there may be such cases. One authority to that effect is the Court of Criminal Appeal decision in *The Queen v Temby* [2003] SASC 230. Debelle J there spoke for the court to that effect at para.21. While the facts of that case are different from this, I think those observations do apply to this case. A judge of this court, in the case of *The Queen v H,SM* [2008] SADC 167, spoke in similar terms about a consensual relationship that there existed between a young man who was 19 and a girl who was 15-and-a-half when a sexual relationship began and continued after the girl turned 16. Again the facts of this case are different, but there, too, the facts were very different from those which normally come before the courts. The sentencing judge drew attention to other cases in this court where the facts of offences of unlawful sexual intercourse have called for merciful sentences.

The prosecution submits that I should impose a prison sentence in this case, albeit that it would be appropriate to suspend it. I agree that that would be the usual approach. Offences of this sort quickly lead to the conclusion that a sentence of imprisonment must be imposed because of the gravity of the offence. That is so notwithstanding that imprisonment is the sentence of last resort. The prosecutor said that the pregnancies increased the seriousness. Normally I would agree with that, too, but in this case the situation is, in my view, different. The complainant was given counselling and contraception after the first termination.

I think that the facts of this case are so far removed from cases which do call for a prison sentence that I should not impose that sentence of last resort. It is not altogether easy to see what penalty I should impose. A fine is not appropriate because you are a student and, at present, do not have any income. It might be thought appropriate to discharge you without penalty upon your entering a bond pursuant to s 39 of the Criminal Law (Sentencing) Act. I think that it could be said that good reason exists for doing so by reason of the circumstances of your relationship with the complainant. However, the purpose of such a bond is usually to ensure that people do not re-offend; they can be brought back to the court to be sentenced if they do re-offend. It might be thought that a bond is necessary to bring home to you that the culture of Australia is very different from Sudan and you cannot have sexual relationships with girls who are under 17 in Australia. However, I believe that the experience of being arrested and charged with rape and facing the proceedings which have followed should be sufficient to bring that home to you.

Further, I note that you propose moving interstate to live. That leaves the question of whether the ultimate leniency can be shown to you by discharging you without penalty, pursuant to s 15 of the Criminal Law (Sentencing) Act. That can only be done where a court finds that the offences are so trifling that it is inappropriate to impose any penalty. That course can be taken with or without recording a conviction. That course can only be taken if, to use the words of the Full Court expressed by Olsson J in *Coles v Catt* (1992) 58 SASR 298 at 308–9:

The court can properly come to the conclusion that it would be manifestly unfair and unreasonable to penalise the offender and to bring about the imposition of the stigma of a criminal conviction.

That course can only be taken where, again using the words of Olsson J: There is a situation that must be so far out of the ordinary or typical case of its type that parliament cannot have contemplated it as falling within the statutory prohibition so as to invoke the full rigour of the law. There must clearly be circumstances that distinguish the case from the general run of its type. I would think that it would almost never be the case that one could characterise the facts of a charge of unlawful sexual intercourse as so trifling as to call for a discharge without penalty and without conviction.

I think the facts of this case, when fully appreciated, do call for that result.

While your ignorance of the law is no excuse, the cultural background of both you and the complainant suggested that sexual relations at 16 were accepted. The fact of the relationship being consensual is irrelevant to the charge of unlawful sexual intercourse, but this was not the case of a predator taking advantage of a vulnerable minor because it was an ongoing relationship going on for 18 months after the complainant turned 17.

Insofar as deterrence is a factor, the fact of your being charged with rape and unlawful sexual intercourse is, I think, enough deterrent for both you and others that sex with minors in Australia is prohibited and is a criminal offence.

While I have not heard evidence of your prospects of employment, I think it likely that the recording of a conviction would make it more difficult for you to get employment in the future. I dismiss the charge without recording a conviction. I do, however, want to make very clear to you that the course I have taken is almost never taken by the courts. This matter will be on your record, even though I have not recorded a conviction. If you were to have sexual relationships with someone else under 17 in the future, no court will show leniency. Sexual relations with people under 17 in Australia is prohibited.

You are free to go.

Mr Jason Collins

Background to the Case

Mr Collins was referred by his lawyer who had been instructed to act for him. The charge of Aggravated Assault causing serious harm was before the County

Court and he was in the process of finalising a plea to this charge on the basis of reckless rather than deliberate intent. The basic facts of the matter were not in dispute. In addition to the usual matters that are covered in a psychological assessment for court, the following specific questions were raised:

1. Is there a relationship between Mr Collins' experience of Aboriginal culture and this type of reactive violence?
2. Could you address some of the literature you have studies and/or authored concerning violence and Aboriginal men as you consider it may relate to Mr Collins' situation.
3. What recommendations would you make as to assisting Mr Collins' to change his behaviour?
4. What is the relationship of alcohol to this type of offending, Does that relate to issues you have found in your research into Aboriginal men and violence?

Background History

Mr Collins reported that he was born in Chinnter, growing up as the second eldest of four boys in the Mirabelle area of Southwark. His mother was the primary carer for the family, although they received a lot of support from their uncles. For Mr Collins, his uncles were *'father figures'* who *'taught us everything — cooking, living, fighting'*. In his words, *'I looked up to them, whatever they done'*. The family moved around quite a lot when he was young and Mr Collins was responsible for looking after his younger brothers from an early age. His father did not live with the family, but some distance away. At the age of 9 or 10 Mr Collins described spending four or five months with his father before returning to Chinter. He described his father as an 'alcoholic' and remembers finding it hard to have a conversation with him.

Mr Collins attended Springton Mission School and enjoyed school, having lots of friends and cousins there. Fighting was an everyday part of school life for all of the students, as well as in the wider community. Mr Collins remembers, for example, how the children would go to watch the uncles fighting after they had been drinking. Although fighting was the normal way of resolving problems, there were some rules in place (e.g., if a child was hurt, *'then the parents would sort it out later'*). He described his brothers as *'bad for fighting'*, and he would fight *'all of the time'* with one brother in particular. Two of his brothers are currently in jail.

Mr Collins continued to attend high school after the family moved to Mount Brook when he was 15 years old. He sees the move to Mount Brook as *'the best move we could have done'* and reported that it was prompted by the need for the boys to find partners outside of their community. Despite getting on well at school ('*I loved school*'), he reported that he did not learn to read or write and would react with aggression when his peers bullied or taunted him about this. He would also intervene when he saw other people being bullied ('*would bash them*'), and gave the example of when he saw a disabled student being bullied. In his words, '*I would always warn people [first]*: '*keep pushing me and I'm gonna bash you*'.

Mr Collins met his current partner when he was 16 years old and they now have five boys of their own, aged from 3 to 14 years. Mr Collins sees his children as '*doing well*', and he takes them to sport at weekends and encourages them to take part in other activities. Some of his beliefs about fighting have, however, influenced his parenting style ('*I teach my kids how to fight — look after themselves*', '*If you don't protect yourself people look at you like a coward*').

Mr Collins is currently in receipt of a disability pension and does not work. He spends his time fixing cars and playing rugby. However, his current lifestyle involves smoking a lot of marijuana to keep calm. He told me that he '*Can't leave the house without out [smoking]*' and that he had to smoke before attending the assessment and was concerned that he would be agitated on his way home after the appointment. Mr Collins reported that he had recently tried to cut down and has started playing rugby league at the weekend. He tries not to smoke on weekends (Saturday when he is playing sport, and Sunday when his children play), but estimates he might smoke an ounce, or an ounce and a half, through the week. For him, this is essential in 'keeping things together': '*when I'm straight I don't want to talk to nobody. I just get angry — about anything. My mind runs at 100 miles an hour and some *** will say something or look at me the wrong way*'. In his view, smoking also helps to stop violent dreams and nightmares. Mr Collins did not report high levels of alcohol use, but said that '*when I go, I go*' and will at these times drink heavily. This will often be when he is feeling happy and he will then relax and socialise ('*everyone comes to my house*'). At other times he feels angry after drinking.

When asked where the anger comes from he replied '*bashed up when I was little*', but did not divulge further details. He reported being very close to his uncles, although over the last year, three uncles have died prematurely and now only one of eight are alive. Mr Collins became tearful when talking about his losses and the responsibility he has now assumed within his family ('*I had to bury them*'). It is important for him to return to his uncle's graves interstate regularly — at these times he thinks, talks to them, and tends their graves with flowers (it '*lets all of my stress out*').

When asked how he copes, Mr Collins spoke about his wide friendship group. He described offering significant levels of support and advice to other people ('*People come to me — I know how to talk*'), but also reflected that there is nobody to support him. His relationship with his mother was previously strong ('*I could talk to her about my problems and she would have an answer, but not since we had a row*'), but has deteriorated markedly following the death of his uncles ('*Mum took it out on all us when an uncle passed away*') and a subsequent argument involving another family member. In order to cope with his feelings, Mr Collins smokes marijuana, spends time in his shed, and plays rugby. He noted that 'taking off' is helpful, but feels unable to leave his house at times because he is worried that it will be damaged.

The Offence

Mr Collins was initial angry and frustrated when he started to talk about the events that led up to the offence. He felt that he had asked a staff member to intervene and that the problem could have been easily resolved if they had responded. At the same time he described feeling ashamed about the offence, knowing immediately that he should not have reacted the way he did ('*I shouldn't have done it*').

On the night of the offence he reported that he had not been drinking heavily, but just returned from an uncle's funeral. Another patron of the club was shouting loudly, which prompted an angry exchange — Mr Collins asked him where he was from and then told him he was not an Australian, being non-Indigenous. He was met with verbal [racial] abuse. The result was one of the staff members escorted Mr Collins out of the club. He remembers feeling controlled (not angry) when walking out of the club, although does remember swearing. He waited outside for his wife, but she was not allowed to leave immediately. When he was subsequently pushed, Mr Collins reacted immediately by punching the staff member. He reported that this was not pre-meditated, rather that it was as response to being touched ('*I don't like to be touched, especially when I'm angry*'). This account is consistent with the police statement of material facts provided to the assessor.

Assessment

Mr Collins attended the assessment with his partner, but was interviewed alone. He was polite and cooperative throughout the interview, and spoke freely about his both history and the current offence. Mr Collins displayed a good level of attention and was able to provide detailed and thoughtful answers to all of the questions posed. His mood changed noticeably through the interview, from anger and frustration when discussing the circumstances of the current offence through to sadness when talking about aspects of his personal and family history. At times in the interview Mr Collins became tearful. He presented as a reliable informant who was providing honest and accurate information to the best of his ability. An interview with his partner provided confirmation of his account of his family history. Nonetheless, this report relies upon self-report which is largely uncorroborated.

Risk of Future Violence

An important goal of any assessment of this type is to understand the extent to which there is ongoing risk of violence to the community. Methods of predicting who will be violent (and who will not) are commonly known as risk assessments. Risk factors are those variables that impact systematically on violence, either by increasing or decreasing its likelihood. Predicting whether someone will commit further acts of violence typically involves establishing which risk factors are relevant to the individual case.

The Historical-Clinical-Risk Management-20 (HCR-20; Douglas, Hart, Webster, Belfrage, & Eaves, 2008) is a structured guide for the assessment of risk of violence among civil psychiatric, forensic, and criminal justice populations. It contains 20 items (10 historical variables, 5 clinical variables, and 5 risk management factors) as well as an item based on the Hare psychopathy checklist (PCL-R). Items are scored as 0 (*not present*), 1 (*possibly present*) or 2 (*definitely present*), yielding a total score out of 40. Variables include relevant past, present, and future considerations.

The 10 items of the Historical (H) scale are primarily static and unlikely to fluctuate over time, they include: (a) previous violence, (b) young age at first violent incident, (c) relationship instability, (d) employment problems, (e) substance use, (f) major mental illness, (g) psychopathy, (h) early maladjustment, (i) personality disorder, and (j) prior supervision failure. The Clinical (C) scale has five items referring to current mental, emotional, and psychiatric status, including dynamic risk markers that are changeable in nature: (a) lack of insight, (b) negative attitudes, (c) active symptoms of major mental illness, (d) impulsivity, and (e) unresponsive to treatment. The Risk Management (R) scale also has five items that are concerned with predicting the future social, living, and treatment circumstances of an individual and anticipating the reactions of the individual to those conditions: (a) plans lack feasibility, (b) exposure to destabilisers, (c) lack of personal support, (d) non-compliance with remediation attempts, and (e) stress.

Mr Collins scored highly on both the Clinical and Risk Management items of this protocol, resulting in an overall risk judgement of **moderate risk of violence**. Although he is not routinely violent, it is possible to imagine a number of scenarios in which provocation will arise and which will lead to impulsive aggression. The main clinical risk factors identified were impulsivity, lack of insight, negative attitudes, and a lack of response to treatment. His plans to manage risk also place him at ongoing risk, given that they appear to lack feasibility (his main methods of risk management are either avoidance or self-medication), he continues to experience stress and de-stabilising events, and lacks personal support. A judgement of moderate risk suggests that a risk management plan should be developed, at the very least including some mechanism for the systematic re-assessment of risk.

Experience of Trauma

The Trauma Symptom Inventory (TSI-2, Briere, 2011) is a measure of post-traumatic stress and other psychological sequelae of traumatic events. It is a 100-item scale that assesses a broad range of psychological symptoms plus intrapersonal and interpersonal difficulties associated with psychological trauma. The test is usually self-administered and is intended for a fifth grade and above reading level, but on this occasion items were read out loud. Items are scored on a 4-point scale with 0 = *never* through to 3 = *often*, and are rated in terms of frequency of occurrence over the previous six months. The TSI has a total of 10 subscales each of which relates to a different aspect of traumatic experience. It also contains three validity scales (which assess atypical responding, inconsistent responding, and response level).

Mr Collins' scores were classified as valid responses to the assessment, and were elevated on 9 of the 10 subscales of the TSI. Scores on two subscales ('anxious avoidance' and 'anger/irritability') in particular suggest that he currently experiences clinically significant traumatic symptoms in these areas. This reflects a marked tendency to avoid situations that he perceives as potentially traumatic, and difficulties in managing anger appropriately.

Wellbeing

The Kessler-10 (Kessler et al., 2003) measure is one of the most widely used assessments for social and emotional wellbeing in the Indigenous community. It asks the respondent to rate how he (or she) has been feeling over the last four weeks. Mr Collins endorsed the ratings 'most of the time' for three items ('feel tired out for no reason', 'feel restless or fidgety', 'feel depressed') and 'all of the time' for one of the ten items ('feel that everything was an effort'). These ratings reflect a high level of dsyphoric emotion and a low level of emotional wellbeing.

Opinion

There are two particular aspects of this assessment that I would like to draw attention to in relation to how Mr Collins' risk of re-offending might be most effectively managed in the future. First, is the influence of attitudes and beliefs that endorse violence and aggression as an appropriate means of resolving conflict. It has been well established that children who observe, or who are subject to, aggressive behaviour in their home environment are much more likely to behave aggressively towards their peers, with this pattern of behaviour continuing into their adult relationships. It is apparent that Mr Collins grew up in an environment in which violence was normalised and has led him to believe that it is important to intervene physically to resolve problems or conflict. These beliefs place him at ongoing risk of acting violently in the future and may be difficult to change. At the same time, however, Mr Collins' violence appears to be largely restricted to circumstances when he perceives some wrong-doing or injustice to have taken place, and often occurs in the context of abuse or discrimination. Indeed, he presents as someone who helps to resolve problems within his community by non-violent means and who is disappointed with himself for reacting the way he did in relation to the current offence.

The second aspect of the assessment relates to the context in which the offence occurred. Mr Collins experiences a low level of wellbeing that is suggestive of trauma. It is difficult to ascertain whether his presentation would fulfil the DSM-5 criteria for Posttraumatic Stress Disorder given the use of marijuana to manage some of these traumatic feelings. It is, however, clear that the loss of his uncles (and consequent lack of support, breakdown in his relationship with his mother, and increased responsibility) has impacted heavily on Mr Collins. Although he seeks to manage this by avoiding stress through substance use, sport, or isolating himself, this has lowered the threshold for when he might react aggressively. In this context, I would see consider his aggression to be impulsive, rather than intentional or planned.

Responses to the following specific referral questions follow.

Is There a Relationship Between Mr Collins' Experience of Aboriginal Culture and this Type of Reactive Violence?

Mr Collins grew up in a remote community that was characterised by violence and alcohol use. It was here that his beliefs about aggression and violence developed, and where he learnt that the only, or most appropriate, way to resolve conflict was through fighting. I would see this as, in part, a consequence of his experience of Aboriginal culture, although it might be better understood as a response to the extreme social disadvantage that he grew up in.

In terms of the relevance of this to the present matter, it has been argued that although the same sentencing principles are to be applied in every case, courts are also bound to take into account all material facts, including those which exist only by reason of the offender's membership of an ethnic or other group (*Neal v R 1982*:326; *R v Fuller-Cust*, 2002). The 'material facts' that have been found to be relevant in sentencing Indigenous offenders include the severe social and economic disadvantage, accompanied by endemic alcohol abuse, which exists in some Indigenous communities. To that end I have reproduced the following text regarding sentencing from an Indigenous Justice Clearing House brief (from Anthony, 2010):

In Fernando (1992), Justice Wood held that the equal treatment of Indigenous offenders required, where relevant, consideration of their subjective circumstances, including their Indigenous background where it threw 'light on the particular offence and the circumstances of the offender' (1992: 62). He stated that where alcohol abuse reflected 'the socio-economic circumstances and environment in which the offender has grown up' it should be taken into account as a mitigating factor (1992:60). He accepted that problems of alcohol and violence 'go hand-in-hand' in Indigenous communities (1992:62). Justice Wood pointed to the need to consider rehabilitation orders because recognition of the relationship between alcohol abuse and violence in Indigenous communities requires 'more subtle remedies' than imprisonment (1992: 62, 63).

The South Australian courts have relied on Fernando in *Ingomar v Police* (1998), *Police v Abdulla* (1999) and *R v Tjami* (2000). In Abdulla, the South Australian Supreme Court held that the Fernando principles should receive 'broad application' beyond 'Aborigines living in the more remote communities' ([34]-[35]), and the Court of Criminal Appeal has noted that these principles were 'not restricted to traditional Aboriginals' (*R v Smith* 2003: [60]).

This case law may be relevant to the Mr Collins' matter in so far as it highlights how the social disadvantage he experienced may be considered in mitigation.

Could You Address Some of the Literature You Have Studied and/or Authored Concerning Violence and Aboriginal Men As You Consider It May Relate to Mr Collins' Situation?

The research I have been involved with in South Australia sought to investigate how anger was conceptualised by a group of adult indigenous male prisoners at Port Augusta prison, the majority of whom had been convicted of, or charged with, violent offences (see Day, Nakata & Howells, 2008). The analysis revealed that participants were generally unable to differentiate between anger and violence. Anger was understood as an uncontrollable emotion, experienced as an irrational process. Often, undifferentiated emotions (e.g., grief, anxiety) were experienced as anger.

While this presentation is somewhat characteristic of violent offenders in general, there were more culturally specific aspects of the findings, especially in relation to the conceptualisation of anger as an emotion that is historically located and inter-generationally compounded by systemic discrimination. Indeed, many of the stories we heard were accounts of early and pervasive violence, which suggested a close link between the experience of anger and experiences of trauma. Indigenous offenders, for example, generally reported more frequent experiences of personal loss or separation, and experiences of traumatic symptoms, particularly associated with inadequate sense of self and personal identity (including problems in discriminating one's needs and issues from those of others, confusion regarding one's identity and goals in life, an inability to understand one's own behaviour, an internal sense of emptiness, a need for other people to provide direction and structure, and difficulties resisting the demands of others).

The results of Mr Collins' assessment resonate with these observations. In my view they lend support for the suggestion that his violence may be best understood as occurring within a context of historical trauma, low emotional awareness, and experiences of perceived discrimination. The implication is that his level of risk may be able to be appropriately managed by addressing problems with emotional recognition and awareness, as well as impulsivity. For any intervention to be effective, however, it will need to be framed from within a broader cultural perspective that identifies and acknowledges traumatic experiences on both a personal and collective level. Grief and loss is the term that is often used to describe this presentation as it is a more powerful explanatory construct than trauma and has cultural significance for many indigenous people in Australia

In simple terms then, this body of theoretical and empirical research suggests that when people experience high levels of psychological distress they commonly fail to regulate their behaviour in the same way as they would in normal circumstances. Their capacity to problem solve and to make effective decisions is diminished. For many Indigenous men these problems are compounded by personal and cultural histories of loss, separation, family dysfunction, and trauma which needs to be acknowledged if interventions are to effectively manage the risk of further offending occurring.

What Recommendations Would You Make as to Assisting Mr Collins to Change His Behaviour?

Given that Mr Collins is assessed as at a moderate risk of acting violently in the future, it is important that effective risk management plans are put in place. In my view there is some scope for some of the clinical risk factors identified in this assessment to be modified through intervention. In particular, if Mr Collins were able to resolve some of the traumatic feelings associated with the loss of his uncles I would see his level of risk as reducing. It is also important to attend to substance use issues, despite Mr Collins' view that it is this which is keeping him calm.

I would suggest a referral to a culturally safe wellbeing program, if one can be identified. A range of potentially appropriate programs are offered through Aboriginal Health services and the Aboriginal Family Support Service has recently launched a new grief and loss program which is in the process of being rolled out across South Australia. Although Mr Collins showed an interest and capacity (in our appointment) to engage successfully in this type of program, he also expressed reluctance to use these services as he knows people at these agencies and would potentially find it difficult to engage, especially as a Koori man. Nonetheless, I would at least recommend a referral to an Aboriginal men's group, if a suitable group can be identified. This would provide support, monitoring and advice as well providing a context in which Mr Collins can work on his recent losses. Supporting Mr Collins to engage with such services would be worthwhile.

Treatment, though, is only one component of risk management and it is also important to consider ways in the ongoing monitoring of risk (e.g., exposure to destabilising experiences, further losses) can occur, possibly through community corrections. A more obvious approach to risk management, perhaps, would be remove him from the community. Mr Collins told me that he considered this a possibility when he next attends Court. In his words '*prison might do me good [I could] get away from it*'. He reported that he knows a lot of people in jail, but also expressed a strong expectation that he would get into fights, especially if he was unable to avoid conflict or self-medicate. Such statements lead me to believe that incarceration would not assist Mr Collins to change his behaviour or, indeed, that there would be great value in implementing sanctions that rely upon with either individual or general deterrence. I would also have some concerns about the wellbeing of his five children if Mr Collins were to be removed from the family.

What Is the Relationship of Alcohol to this Type of Offending, Does That Relate to Issues You Have Found in Your Research Into Aboriginal Men and Violence?
Given the close association between substance use, particularly alcohol use, and offending, it is apparent that Mr Collins' risk of offending would be substantially reduced if his substance use problems were resolved. Although Mr Collins told me that had not been drinking heavily at the time of then offence, the particular issue in relation to alcohol is binge drinking. In our research Indigenous offenders scored higher on a measure of those activities engaged in by an individual as a way to modulate, interrupt, avoid, or soothe negative internal states, and to act out negative affect. We concluded that substance use is one obvious method that many men choose to do this and Mr Collins' presentation is entirely consistent with this observation.

Case Law
Ingomar v Police [1998] SASC 6875
Neal v R (1982) 149 CLR 305
R v Fernando (1992) 76 A Crim R 58 (NSW)
R v Fuller-Cust (2002) 6 VR 496
R v Smith [2003] SASC 263
R v Tjami [2000] SASC 311

Opinion

Mr Arthur Askey

Background to the Case

Mr Askey was referred by his legal aid funded lawyer for a psychological assessment and report to assist in sentencing. Mr Askey had been found guilty on two counts of Attempted Rape, and two counts of Rape, and his lawyer requested that an assessment and report for the court describe Mr Askey's general psychological profile, comment on his state of mind at the time of the offence, and provide an opinion about his current psychological health.

Mr Askey presented as a middle-aged man of average height and solid stature. He was polite, cooperative and articulate throughout the 2½ hour assessment interview, elaborating spontaneously, and he did not refuse to answer any questions directed at him. Mr Askey did not appear to be in distress, and I did not observe any indication that he was experiencing symptoms of psychosis, or any other major mental illness such as anxiety or depression. My observations were corroborated by Mr Askey' self-report, he told me that he had no pressing concerns, and had not sought the assistance of any mental health professionals or counselling support during his imprisonment.

The following sources of information were used in the compilation of this report:

- Clinical interview and psychometric assessment, 5 October 2009
- Letter of referral dated 4 September 2009
- District Court information and allegations
- Statement of the victim, 6 March 2007
- Statement of Forensic Scientist, dated 5 April 2007
- Statement of Forensic Medical Practitioner, dated 7 March 2007
- Mr Askey's Police Offender History Record as at 24 December 2007.

Background History

Family History

Mr Askey reported that he was born in a small town on the remote far west coast, but was removed from his biological family at the age of 6 months by child protection services. He grew up with a foster family in metropolitan Ascot, from the age of 6 months until he was 15 years old. Mr Askey told me that he had older and younger siblings within his foster family, which included a number of biological and adopted children. Mr Askey reported that he was the only child in the household who was fostered and did not share the surname, because '*my Dad wouldn't let them change my name*'. Both his foster parents are now deceased, but Mr Askey told me that he remains in regular contact with his younger brother, who was an adopted sibling, and his closest companion in childhood.

Mr Askey told me that he had learned about his removal from his parents in his late twenties, when he had accessed a child tracing service. He said that he *'wanted to find out everything about myself'*, and had been able to access and read the welfare records in relation to the circumstances of his removal. Mr Askey reported that the official documentation indicated that when authorities had arrived at the family home his mother was not present, and his grandmother was heavily intoxicated. He and another child were reportedly found in a severely neglected state, and were subsequently removed from the home.

Mr Askey reported that he did not get into trouble as a child when he was living with his foster family and *'felt loved but ... felt different'*. Mr Askey's memory of his foster family was that they were *'good'*, but *'very strict ... lots of my school friends were allowed out but I wasn't'* and he was required to attend church and Sunday School. He also described being physically disciplined by his foster parents, to an extent that would today be considered abusive. For example, Mr Askey told me that both he and his siblings were regularly hit with either a belt or a duster, but he also reported a particular incident when he was *'whipped with an extension cord'*, and *'no-one else got the extension cord'*. This occurred when he was approximately 13 and his foster father *'gave me a hiding across my bare back ... I hated him after that'*.

At the age of 15, Mr Askey reported that he started running away from home regularly because he *'wanted to find out who I really was'*. Mr Askey said that he had to go to Youth Court but was still going to school at this time, until eventually when he was 16 *'my foster parents got sick of me'* and he *'went to find my real family'*. At this time Mr Askey said he met someone who *'found my aunty'*, and he stayed with her for a brief period of time.

Mr Askey described himself in his adolescence as *'a drifter'*, telling me that he had lived on the street in the city centre for some time, where he *'made friends and went down the wrong track'*. In his mid-teens Mr Askey made efforts to re-connect with his biological family, and met his father, brothers, sisters and cousins. He reported that he had met his biological mother once, but *'she didn't want nothing to do with me'*, and is now deceased.

Mr Askey said that he first met his biological father when he was 17, but he was disappointed because his father is *'just an alcoholic'*. He told me that his father is *'sick at the moment'*, with cancer, and has *'been told to stop drinking'*. Currently Mr Askey has no contact with his father, telling me that he *'despises'* him, because he *'used to try and beat me up and never showed me any respect'*. He went on to say, *'I tried to do my best by him but I feel they didn't *do right by me ... it makes me angry and still hurts me but the past is the past ... I try to block it out but I know it's still there and it always will be*.

In response to my explicit question about potential experiences of victimisation, Mr Askey disclosed that '*when I finally met my natural family one of my uncles raped me*'. He told me that he had only ever told two people about this before now, those two being '*my best friend*' and '*another bloke once when I was drunk*'. Mr Askey reported that this abuse had occurred when he was '*about 16*', and '*really drunk ... I couldn't do nothing about it*'. He told me that '*it still upsets me to this day ... I still see him too and I don't like him ... he's usually at my aunty's house*'. When I enquired whether he would ever consider pressing formal charges against this man, Mr Askey indicated that he would not because '*I'd feel embarrassed, everyone would hear about it ... I don't want people thinking I'm gay, thinking you're making it up ... I'm the one that has to live with it*'. He also informed me that he has '*thoughts of hurting him all the time but I think of the consequences if I did ... sometimes I feel like I want to kill him but it will only make more trouble for me*'.

Mr Askey reported that he has three children from previous relationships. His eldest daughter, Bronny, is currently in her early twenties, being born when he was approximately 20 years of age. Mr Askey told me that he had a relationship with her mother for approximately three years when he was in his late teens, until '*she was unfaithful in front of me*' and so left, by which time Mr Askey was '*on the run from the courts*'. He later received a message while in jail, and thereby discovered he had fathered a daughter.

By Mr Askey's account he has been '*partially involved*' in her life, telling me that she was raised by a foster mother. He described having visited her once when she was 8 years old, when he and his girlfriend at the time took her out for the day, other than this visitation was '*every now and then*'. Mr Askey told me that he was recently living in the same house with her, her aunty, and her boyfriend, who was reportedly a friend of Mr Askey's.

Mr Askey's second eldest child, Charlie, is currently in his late teens, being born when Mr Askey was approximately 25 or 26 years old. Mr Askey had a 3½ year '*on and off*' relationship with Charlie's mother, which included '*living together in the end*'. Charlie was born during a period of separation, but he was present at the hospital when he was born, telling me that he was '*the only child I got to see as a baby*'. Mr Askey told me that Charlie's mother was '*the wicked witch of the west*', who could be '*nice then nasty*'. However when I asked Mr Askey why his relationship with Charlie's mother eventually ended he said '*I was always coming to prison and getting into trouble ... I was off drugs (except pot) when living with her but drinking a lot ... and she didn't like it*'.

Mr Askey told me that he last saw Charlie when he was 5 years old and he bumped into him out with his grandmother and aunty, but has had no contact at all with him since then. He informed me that the last time he was serving a sentence for armed robbery he was asked whether he would give his permission for Charlie to change his surname but he refused. He stated '*I think <my ex> lies to him about me, I'll follow that up when I get out*'. Mr Askey reported that he wanted to 'prove' to Charlie that he is his father. When I asked how it was that Mr Askey seemed so sure about this, when he had not spoken to any of them for over a decade, he responded '*her sister goes out with a bloke I know*'.

Mr Askey's youngest daughter, Deanna, is currently in early adolescence. He told me that straight after Deanna was born he was sentenced to four years for armed robbery. Mr Askey reported that Deanna's mother '*used to bring her in to visit me for the first three years until she found another bloke and had two kids with him*'. He stated that Deanna's mother has never stopped him from seeing Deanna, and before his recent imprisonment he '*was seeing her all the time, living around the corner from her with my sister*'. However, Mr Askey worries that Deanna's mother '*keeps telling her lies and putting me down*'. Later in the interview Mr Askey expressed his concern that Deanna's mother is an intravenous drug user, and that Deanna is '*already in a drug environment as a kid … there's people in and out of that house using needles … when I get out I would report it to <child protection services> … I don't want her to get involved … I have to think of my daughter*'. While I accepted on face value that Mr Askey's expressed concern was genuine, I also note that such a situation was likely to have been the case for some time, and yet he had not been pressed to act in his daughter's best interests in the past. I advised Mr Askey that should he wish to make a report about this perceived '*high risk environment*' there was nothing to prevent him from doing so while in custody.

Aside from his adopted brother, Mr Askey reported that he also maintains a good relationship with his biological sister who he '*rings all the time*'. He advised that he also has a broad social network of acquaintances and friends who tend to be involved in substance abuse and offending.

Education and Employment

Mr Askey reported that he attended the same primary school from reception to Year 7. He said, in a somewhat contradictory fashion, that he had '*pretty good memories*', but also '*hated school*'. Mr Askey stated that his favourite parts of school were '*sport and recess and lunch*', and he recalled having friends and enjoying playing sport with them. However Mr Askey also said that in years 5 to 7 he was frequently held back after school in detention, on average 2 to 3 times per week, for things like messing around in class, being disruptive, and not doing his homework. He was never suspended or expelled in primary school, however he recounted an incident where he got into trouble for playing on a rope swing at the rear of the school grounds, being sent to the principal's office where he '*got the cane because my parents gave the school permission to hit me*'. Mr Askey said that he '*got the cane so often I got used to it*'.

Mr Askey then attended high school for Year 8. When I reflected to him that he had a broad and eloquent vocabulary he responded '*I was always good at English*'. However his behavioural problems continued to be evident, and toward the end of his first year at high school, following frequent detentions, he told me that he was caught stealing from the school canteen and his mother was called in. Mr Askey told me that he was threatened with expulsion or given the choice to leave voluntarily, and he opted for the latter. After leaving, Mr Askey's foster mother then enrolled him at a specialist school. He reported that this special education facility was '*alright*'. However he did not stay longer than about a year.

Mr Askey reported that he'd had 4 to 5 jobs throughout his life. The first was as a window cleaner, when he was in his mid-20s and in a relationship with the mother of his second child. This job lasted a few months before he was sent back to prison. Mr Askey told me that his second job was working at a company that made garden and soil products. He had obtained this position after gaining his forklift licence from a one-day course organised by government employment services. This job also lasted a couple of months, until Mr Askey and one of his workmates were '*sacked for getting stoned at work*'. Mr Askey reported that he had also done some cash-in-hand work grape pruning in the wine regions for brief periods.

Mr Askey's most recent job, where he was employed at the time of the current offences, was in a factory making air-conditioning products. His role was fork-lift driving in the factory, and he told me that he enjoyed the job, having obtained the position with the assistance of employment services. Mr Askey reported that he was always early for work, but he also acknowledged that he would sometimes take speed before starting, to avoid 'coming down' on shift. At this time he was also reportedly doing some cash-in-hand work through a friend, delivering materials to building sites. Mr Askey said that he was working 5 to 7 days per week and '*loves working*', because it '*gives you independence, you gain money so you don't have to go out stealing, and honest work makes me feel good about myself*'.

Mental Health

Mr Askey recalled having had previous psychiatric and/or psychological reports written about him before, in relation to his armed robbery trial, but he could not remember the details of these assessments. He told me that other than this contact he has never seen any type of mental health professional, because: '*I never felt that I needed to*'. Mr Askey said that he has a few current concerns, such as his children and his pending sentencing, but he did not describe any symptoms of stress, anxiety or depression. He told me that he was, in general, '*not too happy about my life and the way I turned out but I can't blame anyone else ... it still hurts and it always will*'.

Substance Use

Mr Askey reported that he began smoking marijuana and consuming alcohol from the age of 15 years. He then '*got into harder drugs on the street*', including amphetamines, LSD, heroin, cocaine, and '*pills*' (prescription medication). Mr Askey told me that he first used drugs intravenously when he was 17, having become used to watching his companions injecting themselves. In his own words, he '*tried it, liked it, haven't looked back*'.

Mr Askey was able to identify risks associated with his intravenous use of amphetamines, telling me that even after using for over 20 years he still has others inject him because '*I get worried I will f*** it up ... you don't know what can happen ... I've lost lots of friends and family because of needles*'. He described himself as an '*every now and then user*', telling me '*I've seen and been around junkies and I wouldn't put myself in that category, they need it all the time to live a normal life*'. Mr Askey advised me that he has had withdrawals before, indicating a level of physiological dependency associated with regular use, but he dealt with this by '*just riding it out*'. He reported his current use (prior to imprisonment) to be 4 to 5 day binges approximately once a month, occasionally on his own but mostly in the company of other people.

Mr Askey told me that when he has been '*taking pills and drinking alcohol I don't know what I'm doing*'. I note that forensic reports available to me indicate that Mr Askey had alcohol, cannabis, and benzodiazepines in his blood at the time of testing, which I gather was approximately a week after the offence.

With respect to therapeutic intervention, Mr Askey advised me that after he had served his sentence for armed robbery he saw a counsellor regarding his substance use, and found this contact beneficial because it enabled him to '*get a lot of hurt and anger out ... I used to bottle a lot of stuff up ... letting everything out took a lot of weight off my shoulders*'. This ended when his counsellor left the job, and he did not wish to re-engage with someone new.

Offending

Review of Mr Askey's offender history details identified an extensive and varied criminal career, with (so far as I can determine) 110 convictions for a range of offences spanning a 25-year period. Such criminal versatility includes a number of convictions for offences against the person, and use of a weapon, in addition to various theft-related, driving-related, drug-related, and general nuisance type offences.

Mr Askey acknowledged that he had been in prison most of his adult life, and when I sought his own explanation for why this was so, he stated '*I get drunk and get myself into trouble ... I've never been in trouble when I'm sober*'. I felt this was a fairly genuine response reflecting some degree of personal insight, but indicating an overly simplified, somewhat self-serving interpretation of his conduct as an adult. He told me that he copes quite well with imprisonment because '*I'm pretty well known ... I used to be a boxer and made a name for myself on the street*'. Mr Askey stated '*I don't like violence but ... people let people know don't mess with me ... you have to earn your respect*'. He acknowledged '*you win some you lose some, you can't win them all*', but it seemed clear to me that Mr Askey considered himself a member of the prison system's upper echelon. There was a degree of grandiosity in his presentation at this point.

I asked Mr Askey to describe his account of the circumstances surrounding his previous conviction for Indecent Assault just over a decade ago, when he was approximately 28 years old. He made a number of statements about this incident that I felt served to minimise the seriousness of what had occurred, absolve himself of personal responsibility, and attach blame to the 15-year-old female victim. Mr Askey told me '*women lie a lot, even girls I've had children from*'. He explained that he did not contest the charge because he was '*freaked out about being charged with rape*', so he '*did a deal with the prosecution to plead guilty to the lesser charge*' and '*got 8 months*'.

Mr Askey was acutely aware of the potential implications for his safety within prison with respect to such a conviction, and it seemed that his primary concern in regard to this matter was his own reputation. For example, he said '*I always kept it to myself, not even my brother knows, he might take a different view of me if he knew, a lot of people would*'. Mr Askey reported that he was worried that when he is sentenced for the current matter the media might raise his earlier conviction, and '*I may have to be ready to defend myself*'. He told me that he would never go into protective custody if this were the case, saying '*I'd rather die in the process*'.

Mr Askey spoke angrily about the fact that his eldest daughter had been the victim of rape, telling me that he wants to '*get the bloke that did it*', because he had heard that the perpetrator was charged but the charges dropped. He felt that in general, perpetrators of rape '*should be punished*'. It seemed to me that he did not consider himself to be in that category. Mr Askey told me that he had '*only a few*' convictions for violent offences, and when I asked if he thought he had 'an issue' with violence he responded '*of course ... violence gets me in trouble ... <but> sometimes violence gets me my* own way ... I know it's not good to think like that but in my world some people don't listen to words'. I believe that this statement indicates a degree of ambivalence about his conduct that should be the focus of future intervention attempts.

Mr Askey told me 'over the years I have learnt how to control my anger and a lot of things ... I think of the consequences of my actions'. He advised me that he had completed low-intensity correctional rehabilitation programs multiple times. Mr Askey also reported that when he was coming to the end of his sentence for Indecent Assault and was housed in a pre-release centre with access to day release he had attended a community-based sexual offender treatment program 'a few times', but this had ended when he was sent to a regional prison for 'allegedly' dealing drugs within the pre-release centre.

While excusing some of his earlier adolescent offending (e.g., 'I was learning to survive'), Mr Askey expressed sentiments acknowledging his own breach of societal norms, saying 'I've done a lot of wrong bad things ... I feel sorry for them ... I do have remorse ... I wish I could change it, but ...'. When I queried what he felt he needed to change to prevent future re-offending, Mr Askey's initial response of 'I don't know', was followed by 'drugs and alcohol, I would change the way I carry on sometimes'. He stated that he believed he had 'slowed down a bit more recently', and was 'getting a bit more wiser'. Later in the interview when the topic of personal change re-emerged, Mr Askey reiterated that there are not really any aspects of himself that he would like to change, telling me that while he 'hates a lot of things' about what he has been through, he is also grateful that these experiences have made him who he is. He said, 'in my own mind it's too late to change back to the old world' (meaning the pro-social community within which he was raised), 'all of my associates are going to keep me connected to this world'. Again, he expressed ambivalence that should be further explored therapeutically, acknowledging that these choices were 'not entirely out of my control', but expressing hesitation, 'I don't think I'd fit in'.

This social-self-construct, 'fitting in', seems to me to be central in the aetiology of Mr Askey's personality development and associated prolific offending behaviour. With regard to pro-social ties within the community (which may constitute a protective factor against re-offending), Mr Askey told me that he looks up to extended family members who are footballers.

Sexual History

In addition to the three relationships described earlier, Mr Askey also reported many short-term relationships and one-night-stands, 'more than I can count'. He told me that he masturbates on average 2 to 3 times per week and fantasises about previous sexual relationships at these times. Mr Askey described his ideal relationship as 'with someone who thought like me and did *things like me, that had respect and trust'*. He stated that he had paid for sex once, at a brothel in another capital city, following his second professional boxing fight. Mr Askey said that he had been to strip clubs before but *'it's not something I usually do ... if you've seen one woman naked you've seen them all, they might be different shapes and sizes but it's all the same to me'*.

Account of the Current Offences

Mr Askey told me that at the time the current offences occurred he had been out of prison for approximately five years, in his words, *'a long time ... a record'*. He was working at a factory for approximately three months and using drugs and alcohol on a regular basis, including before going to work on some occasions. In Mr Askey's opinion the main contributing factor to him *'keeping straight'* during this time was his children, and the fact that he was *'thinking about them ... catching up with them and getting to know them ... I didn't want to be off my face around them, I wanted them to see me for who I am and not what their mothers' were telling them'*. From his perspective, *'things were going well'* for Mr Askey at the time of the offences, he was *'seeing a girl'*. He had *'met <the victim> the night before'* the offence, and in his mind *'she was coming onto me then'*.

Mr Askey reported that on the day of the offence he saw his then-girlfriend *'in the bedroom with another bloke'*, which triggered a verbal altercation, and she kicked him out of the house. He said that he then took his bags to his sister's house. He spent the day *'just hanging out and partying ... smoking dope and drinking'*. Mr Askey informed me that he intended to appeal his conviction because he felt that he was innocent, and could not see how he was found guilty. He stated, *'there was no DNA evidence ... no injuries ... she was unsure of anything ... and I know I didn't do it'*. When asked to describe his recollection of the evening in question, Mr Askey told me that he and the victim had been drinking together, that the victim had then given him some Serepax (a prescription benzodiazepene) and *'after that I blacked out'*.

Mr Askey went on to make several statements which served to denigrate the victim of the offence; for example, *'she's a drug dealer, she sells marijuana, there's people coming in and out of that house all day, but that wasn't brought up in court ... you can't trust a woman like that'*. He also stated *'I've got female friends who've known her for years ... it's not the first time she's done this, I'm not her first victim'*, and expressed the opinion that the victim was motivated by financial compensation. When I asked Mr Askey if he thought women in general often make false allegations of rape he replied, *'of course'*. Such statements indicate an adherence to stereotypical rape myths.

Despite his denial that he'd had sexual intercourse with anybody on that night, Mr Askey also made further statements that I felt served to justify and minimise the seriousness of the offence in question. For example, Mr Askey said to me '*she was sitting on my lap, she was all over me ... her best friend could verify that, she was sitting across the table from us saying 'get a room' ... I had my hand down her pants and top and she wasn't complaining, if she didn't want to be in that position she could have said stop*'. When I asked Mr Askey if he thought this meant the victim was consenting to sexual intercourse he replied '*most probably*'. Such cognitive distortions represent important antecedents to sexual offending, and thus would be the target of intensive psychological intervention programs such as those offered by the Department for Correctional Services.

Future Plans

Mr Askey advised me that has spent 18 months on remand for the current offences, and is anticipating that the sentence he might receive will '*most probably be a long time*'. He commented '*it's out of my hands ... <but> this report might help me*', and he intended to use his sentence to '*get to education*'. Mr Askey said '*I made one slip up ... I know I won't do it again*', which in my opinion was a gross minimisation of his offending, both in this particular instance, and in general. I did believe that Mr Askey was genuine in his intention to avoid re-offending, as he told me that he would be '*trying my hardest to make sure I don't come back ... at my age I've seen enough ... I know I need to put a full stop to it and I know I will, no matter what anyone else says*'. Such commendable goals however are unlikely to see fruition without intensive psychological rehabilitation, and Mr Askey's views on this seemed mixed (e.g., '*I'm willing to comply with anything <such as treatment recommendations> ... but at the end of the day I'm the only one who can help myself*'). His goals for the future were to '*get out and get employment ... be a responsible father and try to prevent them going down the same road ... be loving, caring and sharing and all that ... <and> have a good demeanour and be a good person*'.

Assessment

Risk Assessment

Actuarial measures of risk function by placing individual offenders into groups with known reconviction rates, so that individual risk estimates are based on observed group outcomes. The Static-99, a risk assessment measure utilising historical offence-related variables, identified Mr Askey as at high risk of re-offending. His score is associated with observed rates of sexual re-offending of 13.4% for routine samples of sex offenders and 27.7% for high-risk samples at 5 years post-release, and 16.7% for routine samples and 37.3% for high-risk samples at 10 years (see Helmus, Hanson, & Thornton, 2009).

The Stable 2007 was used to further inform this judgement. This is a structured professional judgement tool that has five sections, requiring ratings of Significant Social Influences; Intimacy Deficits; General Self-

Regulation; Sexual Self-Regulation; and Co-Operation With Supervision. Each section is scored up to a total of 2 points, with total scores then categorised as 'low', 'moderate', or 'high' risk. The total score for Mr Askey placed him within the high-risk range. Areas of particular concern were intimacy deficits and general self-regulation, which should be considered to constitute primary targets for rehabilitation and risk management.

Opinion

The following opinion and recommendations are based on the background materials available and information provided during clinical interview, as described earlier. I formulate my summary in response to your specific referral questions.

General Psychological Profile

Mr Askey's early development was characterised by physical and probable emotional neglect as an infant, necessitating his removal from the care of his biological parents at 6 months of age. Such critical early experiences can contribute to an individuals' attachment style, which is a particular style of relating to significant others that can remain stable across the life-course, thought to be affected by both in-born temperament and environmental factors. Children with poor attachment often have difficulty trusting parental figures, and people in general, and thus can have great difficulty forming protective bonds, even when placed in stable foster families. Other children in the same foster family who might have a more functional attachment 'style' may be able to adapt better. The fact that Mr Askey was the apparent recipient of the most severe physical punishment would no doubt have exacerbated his sense of exclusion, of not truly belonging, and thereby laid the foundation for a pervasive sense of loneliness, rejection, and probably fear, which then during his adolescence seems to have expressed itself in resentment, and anger, at the true injustice of his early life experiences. Mr Askey's 'acting out' behaviour as a child would seem characteristic of these early difficulties.

Adolescence is a critical period of psycho–social development, when individuals seek to establish a sense of themselves, and where they fit in the world. Physical and sexual abuse, and rejection by his biological parents probably further exacerbated Mr Askey's ever-growing sense of disconnection from others, and a general dissatisfaction with the world at large. He began, like those around him, to seek the oblivion of substance abuse as a way of coping with the harsh realities of the world he had become a part of, and has maintained heavy poly-substance use for over 25 years. In such situations it is not uncommon for individuals to develop what are commonly called entrenched anti-social attitudes, essentially the view that one must look out for oneself because no-one else will, and therefore one's own self-interest becomes super ordinate to the rights and wishes of others. Mixing in peer groups and sub-cultures where such views are shared serves to strengthen the impact of such beliefs upon an individual's behaviour.

Using the terminology of psychiatric models of human experience, Mr Askey would satisfy diagnostic criteria for Anti-Social Personality Disorder and a Substance Abuse Disorder. He was assessed to be at high risk of sexual re-offending.

State of Mind at the Time of the Offence

I believe a number of distal and proximal antecedent factors in combination contributed to Mr Askey's offending on this occasion. Predisposing psychological features include entrenched anti-social beliefs and adherence to stereotypical rape myths (e.g., women ask for it, women are liars, etc.), along with a sense of entitlement and long-standing pattern of asserting his own needs over the rights of others. These fairly stable features of Mr Askey's personality would probably have been triggered by the event of witnessing his girlfriend talking to another man in the bedroom and then being kicked out, a situation which I gather left Mr Askey feeling angry, resentful, outraged and humiliated.

Pre-existing deficits of emotional and behavioural self-regulation were then further exacerbated by the disinhibiting effects of drug and alcohol use, such that any tenuous internal cognitive barriers to sexual offending would seem to have been readily overcome.

Current Psychological Health

With regard to Mr Askey's current psychological health, I did not observe any indication that he was experiencing symptoms of psychosis, nor any other major mental illness such as anxiety or depression, nor transient states such as acute distress. My observations were corroborated by Mr Askey's self-report, he told me that he had no pressing concerns, and had not sought the assistance of any mental health professionals or counselling support during his imprisonment.

As stated earlier, I believe that Mr Askey could be described as having a severe antisocial personality disorder and a substance use disorder (historically), and both of these have a significant impact upon his risk of future reoffending, be it a sexual offence or any other type of offence. I recommend that Mr Askey be assessed by Correctional Services to participate in the intensive rehabilitation program which they provide. This service is best placed to determine which specific programs, and in which sequence, would be most appropriate for Mr Askey.

Court Outcome

Mr Askey received a reasonably lengthy custodial sentence (7 years non-parole period, with 4 years parole) and was then referred through to the prison sexual offender treatment program. The sentencing District Court Judge placed significant emphasis on the psychological report in his sentencing remarks commenting that 'a psychological report showed Askey had no regret for the rape and made derogatory comments about the victim ... the report says you have a severe anti-social personality disorder'. The report was considered important to the rationale for the judge's sentencing decisions.

Chapter 4

Going to Court as an Expert Witness

Every forensic evaluation that a psychologist accepts to conduct is one that has the potential to go to trial. Every one — even though in the end only a small percentage of cases proceed to a full trial needing your assistance. With this in mind, the psychologist, from the outset, tries to craft an opinion and report that is designed to be 'bullet proof' or one built with an empirical foundation that is hard to contest. So preparing for a court appearance begins with the acceptance of the file — finding out the legal questions that are pertinent and gathering data that will address these issues in an objective fashion. Some criminal files have a higher probability of a full trial such as when the question involves the legal culpability of the accused in a serious crime but others, such as a pre-sentence report are much less likely to require cross-examination in a court appearance.

When a case is accepted, potential trial dates or appearances should be canvassed and noted in the file to ensure that the expert is available for these. Sometimes a trial date looms very quickly and the psychologist will have to consider whether he or she can produce a report within the timelines given. An adjournment may have to be sought in a complex case that will require comprehensive testing and gathering of third party information to inform the opinion.

It is vital for the forensic examiner to understand the evidence presented in a criminal case, for if they are presented with material they have not seen while giving testimony, there is always a possibility that the opinion thought to be based on solid ground may be not as stable as believed. Lawyers will often inquire when referring a case — 'what do you need' — and the psychologist should outline the scope of the data required, including prosecution disclosure of the charges against the accused and the supporting witness statements or other primary evidence. Preliminary hearing transcripts are useful to read as they report witnesses of fact statements under the scrutiny of cross-examination. These can later be placed before the accused for their comment or rebuttal. Providing the expert with full supporting information is the responsibility of the retaining lawyer, but it is the expert with egg on his or her face if this occurs!

In each report, the author should acknowledge that they understand the material in their report may be adduced in evidence in the legal matter and therefore accepts that there is a potential for them to be cross-examined on the issue. They should also indicate that the accused understood that the information had the potential for presentation in court. In many jurisdictions there is no proprietary hold on expert witnesses in criminal cases — if retained by the defence; for example, they can be questioned informally by the prosecution (and vice versa) after a report has been completed but prior to any court appearance. The questions asked may simply be clarification of an issue or fact raised in the report, and such inquiries often satisfy the opposing counsel and prevent an appearance in court. This contact also satisfies the neutral stance that the expert must assume, in the report and on the witness stand. In the case, where there is no report rendered the prosecution may ask for a verbal or short written 'will say' statement.

Know the Legal Landscape

Experienced forensic evaluators will be well aware of the clash of paradigms between sciences such as psychology and the criminal justice system. Language and culture are different and anyone new to acting as an expert needs to learn about the law just as if they were visiting a foreign land (Haney, 1980). The word 'reliability', for example, has a well-honed and specific meaning in psychology, but in law it is usually translated as dependable — is the evidence reliable? Knowing such details and explaining them in court sets you as a knowledgeable visitor to the land of the law. Knowing the key legal cases in the jurisdiction where you are giving evidence will raise the status of your opinion.

Once a report has been entered as an exhibit or agreed to be so by both parties, either side can also offer to produce the expert to give viva voce ('in the live voice') evidence. When the psychologist is contacted regarding their availability for such testimony estimates of time required will be discussed. These estimates are invariably too short. The wheels of justice do grind slower than most of us would like and it is prudent to allow generous overbooking of time for court appearances. Days, not hours, may be required to provide testimony and fidgeting on the stand because you are going to be late for an appointment back at your office or that your parking meter is about to expire does not add to the focus needed for this role.

Being an expert witness is not a volunteer position — you are asked or required to attend court. Sometimes this is accomplished informally — you are asked to attend and arrive there promptly when you are asked to. Other psychologists insist on receiving a subpoena (Latin for 'under penalty') or formal notice to attend a trial. This is sometimes required if the psychologist is employed by a public institution such as a forensic evaluation service or university and casts the appearance as a legal 'duty'. Those who are issued with a subpoena are required to respond or else risk being found in of contempt of court.

Pre-Trial Consultation

After the report has been sent to the referring party and it is decided that court testimony from the psychologist will be required, it is recommended that a consultation with the lawyer be arranged to review the scope of the intended testimony. With a lawyer who is well known to the psychologist and the area of testimony well defined, this may not be necessary but it is usually always helpful, even if it is only a briefing over the phone. During the consultation, it is helpful to go over your curriculum vitae, pointing out highlights that may be germane to the case at bar. Some psychologists actually prepare a question and answer document for the lawyer to guide them through the qualification stage of the trial. You, of course, should always reiterate your purpose in attending court — to be of assistance to the trier of fact (judge or jury) and as an educator. You will draw on your own observations from the case — your interview with the accused, psychological testing, and all the documentation and third party information that contributed to your formation of an opinion. As a teacher, you can readily draw on the science of psychology as it relates to the case — what has psychology to say about this diagnosis, this behaviour, or this act? Obviously, the information that you present may assist one side more than the other in their interest in the matter — prosecution or defence. However, that should never matter to an expert who will answer each question without regard to its impact on either side.

Preparation

In preparing to give evidence the psychologist should let the lawyer know which of his or her qualifications are most important and then discuss a structure of the testimony beginning with a description of the assessment and the results of the evaluation. Opinions should be stated clearly, not in a hesitant or wishy-washy fashion.

More time should be spent preparing for cross-examination than for the direct examination (sometimes called the examination-in-chief), which is essentially an oral summary/extension of the report. There are always some questions that could be asked of any psychologist in cross-examination and experienced forensic evaluators become adept at seeing how these might be used to their own work. An alternative is to have a colleague prepare a set of questions that might be asked in the cross-examination. Having a set of ready responses will give the expert more control over the process. Rarely will the cross-examiner be able to see all the potential issues at play unless they have retained an expert to help them formulate questions. This is far more common in civil litigation (as there is a larger purse to pay for such expertise) than in criminal cases. Nonetheless, a good expert is a prepared expert. You should know the facts of the case cold — memory experts suggest that preparation should take place shortly before testimony — not three months in advance.

We advocate dressing formally for courtrooms — dark suits and conservative attire — this reflects the atmosphere of the courtroom and again signals that you mean business. You should bring to court any material you think necessary — such as your report, any articles you may refer to, and so on. Be aware, however, that anything you take to the stand is discoverable. The lawyer cross-examining you can ask to see all of the materials in your briefcase. If you bring raw test data to court this can become problematic. While not a common problem, a lawyer cross-examining you may look at the 25-page computerised print out from a personality questionnaire and ask you why you left some of the material out of your report — or a lawyer may look at a graph, even giving it to a judge and try to interpret it without any knowledge of what a standard deviation is. It is within our experience to have a judge question psychological test scores by saying it is obvious that one score is greater than another when indeed there is no statistical difference. You do not necessarily have to bring your entire clinical file unless you are served a subpoena duces tecum that should clarify which documents you are compelled to bring with you to the court.

Getting Qualified or 'Proofed' as an Expert

Arrive early at the courthouse and be sure what courthouse you are scheduled for — major urban centres often have more than one building for different levels of court. A list of trials and the room location is posted or on overhead screens at the courthouse. Find that room and wait outside. Sometimes experts can wait in the courtroom but it is uncomfortable to be asked to leave if this is not the case for you. When you are called into the courtroom, walk confidently to the stand. Some courtrooms have witness boxes where you can only stand, but in others you may sit. While this is a personal preference, a more powerful presence will be given if you stand. You will be asked your name and how it is spelled. Then the oath is administered. This ancient tradition has deep roots in most religions and was a natural to be used in courtrooms to increase the validity of testimony. In modern times, the oath is sworn on a sacred book, most often the Bible, which is held in the right hand or with the right hand resting on the book. In many United States' jurisdictions the left hand is placed on the Bible with the right hand held palm forward. The oath is read by a clerk and the expert is to reply. If you observe another religion and wish to swear an oath on sacred writings from that you should bring it with you. A solemn affirmation without religious reference can be substituted for an oath in nearly all jurisdictions. Knowingly falsifying testimony under oath that could influence the outcome of a trial is a criminal offence (perjury).

You will be introduced to the court by the lawyer who called you, and he or she will indicate the purpose of your testimony and ask that you be deemed an expert for this purpose. This often takes place in a voir dire ('to speak what is true') — a technical procedure to ensure that the witness is indeed qualified before having the evidence registered. The judge must rule on your status as an expert after hearing your qualifications. It does not matter how many times you have given evidence — you must be qualified on each appearance. All psychologists would be deemed experts as their knowledge is much above that of the average person.

You should always bring multiple copies of your curriculum vitae (CV) even if you have provided such to the lawyer along with your report. In the pile of paperwork, these can be mislaid and having extra copies ready for the court to peruse is a sign of your preparation. The lawyer will take you through your CV and, with your prior advice, will know what to emphasise. Experts are named such on the basis of knowledge, skill, training, education, and experience. These are therefore the areas to cover in the qualification stage. The CV should be entered as an exhibit so that the judge or jury can peruse it while deliberating. A judge will often follow along during qualification while the lawyer leads the expert through their CV. A CV should outline the current and past clinical/academic positions held, formal education and degrees, professional registrations and societies, honours, appointments, applied experience, teaching responsibilities and then detail lectures given and a full listing of publications of the expert. An experienced expert will also list prior cases in which they gave testimony. With a lengthy CV and a seasoned expert, the opposing counsel may offer to forego this process and accept the witness, knowing they are going to be accepted anyway. The lawyer who retained you will resist this kindness, knowing that the opposing counsel does not want all of your wonderful accomplishments to be highlighted. However, it will be painful if the lawyer decides to go through your 20-page CV line by line. Instead, an effective approach to entering your qualifications is to use a general narrative approach — 'Doctor, can you describe your university education and training'. The length of time you have been in practice, number of cases evaluated, number of times admitted as an expert (at which level and what jurisdictions) and any specialty designations are important to identify as they add weight to your expertise.

Publications are important to highlight as they set you as a scholar as well as clinician. If there is a specific publication of yours on the issue at hand then identify it and discuss the findings or conclusion of the paper. The lawyer offering you as an expert should be prepared to highlight your amazing awards and accomplishments while your evidence on your professional life should be more factual. If the expert introduces accolades of their professional life, it may appear rather self-aggrandising. As an example, if you have been named a Fellow of a national organisation of psychologists, the judge or jury will not know what this means. The lawyer may introduce meaning to this title by reading from the organisation's literature — 'as I understand it this designation is voted upon by your peers across the country and recognises a significant contribution to the science and profession of psychology'. The lawyer adding that the honour is bestowed on less than 1% of the profession adds weight without the expert appearing narcissistic. The opposing counsel may have a few questions about your qualifications and may have even gone to the effort of finding prior judgements about your evidence, so you should know the specifics of these as well. If you ordinarily are retained by the defence rather than prosecution, the latter may ask about this imbalance but do not be defensive on this point. These imbalances are most commonly a result of referral practices and not any actual bias by the witness. Your response should indicate that you answer the door regardless of who knocks. It is helpful to have experience testifying for both sides in criminal cases.

The Scientific Expert

Sometimes a behavioural expert is called to give testimony without conducting an evaluation of an accused. Generally, less weight is given to such experts but they can be very valuable in criminal trials to explore the scientific foundation of an issue critical to a trial. There is a litany of subjects in behavioural science that can be relevant — the effects of alcohol and drugs; cognitive functions such as memory and attention and how reliable these are (or are not) in eyewitnesses; the effectiveness of different types of interventions for various mental disorders; specific issues with aboriginal offenders; the nature of rape trauma syndrome; disputed confessions; methodologies of police investigations with child witnesses — to name a few. Of course, reference to a scientific issue in a clinical forensic report (including appropriate footnotes) is becoming more common, but the purely scientific expert typically has specific expertise in an area and likely has published relevant material as well. The role of the scientific expert is typically just educational and making comments specific to the case must be done cautiously if at all. Not all such evidence will be allowed, however. Supreme Courts and other federal regulatory statutes have set specific criteria for the acceptance of expert evidence. Ordinarily this challenge does not occur but if an expert introduces novel scientific information or give evidence that does not reach outside the knowledge of the average person, the opinion may be rejected by law. The court may decide that the evidence is not necessary, the expert is not qualified to give an opinion on the subject or that it may be unusually prejudicial. Specific criteria for inclusion of expert evidence are covered in our chapters on specific jurisdictions.

Examination in Chief

Direct examination begins after you have been qualified as an expert by the lawyer. Begin by outlining what the mission of the assessment was as directed by the referring party. The organisation of the report and testimony is to describe, first — the history of the accused, the nature of the psychological tests given and then interpret what the findings are and what it means to the case issues. Psychological tests should be demystified as empirical and structured samples of behaviour rather than litmus tests for a disorder and never as an indication of a legal finding (e.g., insanity). When asked about the weight of information obtained, most forensic psychologists reply that their interview and personal experience with the accused has more impact than less direct measures of the accused's behaviour although all information can be important in formulating an opinion of use to the court. For further information about the forensic interview a recent book (Nesca & Dalby, 2013) provides in-depth review of issues the clinician should be aware of.

A psychological report prepared pre-trial may not necessarily be entered as evidence. A trial is about oral evidence and written reports are often thought of as simply a way to refresh the memory of the witness. However, if both sides agree the report can be entered as an exhibit — the law on this is very mixed depending on jurisdictional practices. We prefer psychological reports go in as evidence as it is a substance of the subsequent opinion and may contain details not necessarily explored in full in oral evidence. Of course, in a pre-sentencing hearing, the entering of a written report as an exhibit is very common as expert oral testimony is often not required.

Although it might seem strange to do so at first, your answers should be directed to the trier of fact — the judge or jury. Speaking to the jury by looking at them not only establishes your experience, but sets up a connection between them and you. The same applies to interaction with a judge when he or she is sitting alone. During later cross-examination, a lawyer may walk to the opposite side of the room away from a jury to interfere with the connection you have made with them.

Like the qualification stage of examination, the direct examination flows best with a free narrative from the expert with minimal guideline questions set by the lawyer. A simple question about how you went about assessing the accused and what the results are is all that is needed for an experienced expert. The expert will tell the 'story' of the evaluation and then show how this is relevant to the legal question(s) that were put to him or her. The story model of evidence has been found to be the most appropriate for jurors and judges to comprehend and recall later. The information must logically flow rather than be fragmented pieces of information.

Whether the expert addresses the ultimate issue in a case is a matter of debate. Older schools of thought support a conservative approach that eschews such intrusions into the domain of the trier of fact (see Rogers & Ewing, 2003; Tillbrook, Mumbley, & Grisso, 2003 for both sides of the argument), however, appellate courts have generally concluded that it is not improper for an expert to discuss the ultimate issue with the realisation that the decision still rests with the trier of fact.

What is not up for debate is 'oath helping' which is making direct comments about the truthfulness of the accused in his statements or defence. Appellate courts have repeatedly confirmed that this is the sole domain of the courts — experts cannot offer opinions of credibility but only character.

Cross-Examination

After the direct examination, you are asked to answer any questions that the opposing lawyer might have. Although you are objective and have presented information in this way, do not for a minute consider that you are among friends. While some lawyers cross-examine experts in a dispassionate fashion others take the 'adversarial' approach very seriously and consider it their duty to literally destroy your evidence. This is typically an ineffective method with an experienced expert who could respond in a strong and assertive manner and actually flip questions back on the cross-examiner. Maintaining a courteous demeanour in the midst of an attack is difficult but increases your credibility and addressing your cross-examiner by his or her name is often disarming.

If you understand your data and the substance of your opinion as laid out in your report then you should readily be able to predict the scope or even specific areas of weakness where cross examination will likely focus. Experienced experts often prepare cross-examination questions — along with their responses — prior to trial and relay that they always think of more cross examination questions than they are ever asked.

If at all possible try to have cross-examination completed on the same day as the direct examination. Discuss this with the lawyer who retained you.

Courts have determined that cross-examination must proceed in a timely fashion after the direct examination but if the opposing lawyer has a weekend or more to prepare for cross-examination this is to your disadvantage.

The cross-examination often will focus on the sufficiency of the evaluation. Was an-hour-and-a-half interview with the accused sufficient to gather all the relevant material to reach a conclusion? The answer always has to be that enough time was taken to address the questions posed and an evaluation using twice or three times the amount of time would not have added value to the outcome. Lawyers comparing different experts will try to suggest that because one expert took more time or had more interviews with the accused that their opinion is superior in some way. There is no empirical evidence to support such a hypothesis. Indeed, some have argued that criminal forensic evaluations must be focused only on the questions relevant and may not be 'comprehensive' in the sense of canvassing or testing every aspect of an accused's life. Taking a detailed sex history from a person not accused of a sex crime may not only be unnecessary but may be questioned as to the ethics of that inquiry. It is our experience that comparing the length of time two opposing experts took in interviewing an accused is likely not a critical issue. More experienced interviewers are in fact likely take less time than novices in their interviews.

Tests used by psychologists will be challenged and their accuracy questioned. An understanding and evaluation of potential malingering or other response distortion should be expected to be reviewed. It is important to understand the technical structure of the tests used and the strengths and limitations for forensic work. Reviews of such applications for the MMPI-2 (Otto, 2002; Pope, Butcher, & Seelen, 1993); MCMI-III (McCann, 2002) and even the Rorschach (Gacono, Evans & Viglione, 2002) are available. Specific applications of the PAI for forensic work are beginning to accumulate as well (Kucharski, Petitt, Toomey, & Duncan, 2008; Boccaccini, Murrie, & Duncan, 2006). Some lawyers will try to undermine the evidence with technical questions that very few forensic psychologists would know. For example, a question about the statistical properties of t scores and their development in a specific test may be difficult to recall. Instead, a psychologist can by analogy compare the expert use of tools by other professions (e.g., professional race car driver) with the technical underpinnings of their tool (e.g., what is the exact spark plug gap in their vehicle). It is the skilled use of the tool in the appropriate setting that should be tested. A search for trivial knowledge indicates to the expert that the cross-examiner has little of substance to test.

There are a number of typical cross-examination approaches that are easy to spot and deflect. The repetition of the same question is frequent and there is no difficulty with you stopping that by saying, 'I have already answered that question and my answer will remain the same no matter how many times you ask it'. The objection from your corner should be 'asked and answered'. Another tactic is demanding that you answer only 'yes' or 'no' to a question. You can forcefully explain that you have taken an oath to tell the 'whole' truth and since this cannot be done with a 'yes' or 'no' you must by oath be more comprehensive or refuse to answer in a constricted way. Judges will not allow lawyers to impede witnesses' evidence in this way. Do not be bullied:

- If you are asked a question and you want to refer to some of the material you brought with you, it is proper to ask the judge if this would be acceptable. It is acceptable to 'refresh your memory' by looking at your prior notes.
- You can be asked 'hypothetical' questions as an expert but be clear in responding that if any other information is added or subtracted then you cannot guarantee that your response would be the same. Hypothetical questions are most often used when the facts is a case are in dispute so you are giving evidence on a case that might be similar to some of the issues in the case at bar.
- Always hesitate a moment before answering a question in cross-examination — this gives your counsel the opportunity to object to the question and it may be withdrawn. Be sure to have the lawyer finish their question before answering and do not try to anticipate the question half way through. Always stick to answering only the question rather than venturing into other territory. If a long compound question is asked — comment that the question needs to be broken down into several shorter ones for you to answer. Asking the cross-examiner to repeat the question is always acceptable and we have seen lawyers forget what they asked when a long question is presented. You can always ask for clarification of a question as well.

Most psychological experts have pockets of strong expertise while having less knowledge in other areas. These natural variations in knowledge are found in every type of expert. If an area of cross-examination falls outside your high expertise level then you will be allowed to testify on it (as you have been qualified and have more knowledge than the general public) but may go to the weight given to the particular opinion on that specific information. If cross-examination is a long one and a break is necessary, it is important to remember that you cannot discuss the case with anyone during this period.

A host of approaches to cross-examination are possible. One is to ask a variety of often irrelevant questions to which you do not know the answer. Openly acknowledging that you don't know the answer to a question does not diminish your testimony. This is a tactic to upset novice witnesses. Many experts use internal self-talk to control their emotional reaction or to calm themselves in the middle of testimony.

The lawyer who is cross-examining you may refer to a noted expert in the field who has published some work contradicting your opinion. You should ask to see such work and be given time to review it. The question is often withdrawn if you ask for this or if you are given it, the material has, more often than not, been misquoted or misinterpreted. If you are effective in rebutting such attacks effectively the length of the cross-examination is likely to be shortened since you have become a dangerous witness to try to manipulate.

Re-Direct

Following the end of cross-examination, the lawyer who presented you as an expert is afforded an opportunity to ask follow-up questions about material raised in the cross-examination. The lawyer who retained you may wish to repair any damage done to his or her case by fleshing out some of the answers you provided in cross-examination. Again, the expert is not there to help one side but simply to answer honestly the questions put to him or her.

Post-Trial Consultation

After the testimony is finished, your future preparation continues. You should spend a few minutes with counsel who called you, or other observers, about what went well in the testimony and what did not. If the trial continues after your appearance, call the patient's lawyer after it has concluded. Consider the cross-examination an education about the process. Even after hundreds of occasions testifying in court there is always something to learn so that your performance as an expert will always continue to improve. Professional sports players have coaches and trainers yet they are among the best players in the world. To remain so they have accepted the continuous education model and so should you. Find out the result of the trial you participated in and if the judge had any comments about your testimony. A conviction of the patient when you were appearing for the defence does not reflect badly on you — your testimony is often not the deciding factor. It is natural for you to think of better answers to questions asked after you have left the stand but, with time, your off the cuff responses on the stand will become sharper and more powerful. Do not dwell on your performance; the trial is not about you after all. In high profile criminal trials, you may be approached by media for comment, but you should resist making any comments to media. It is fine to comment on criminal cases you are not involved in as long as the comments are general and not directed to questions of guilt.

Advanced Performance

Some psychologists who regularly appear in courtrooms develop skills that have been studied for their effectiveness. Drawing on their own experiences in the courtroom as well as social science literature, Bank and Poythress (1982) described elements that increase the persuasiveness of the expert witness. Once you have been presented as an informed, trained, able, intelligent and authoritative professional by review of your credentials it is time to show it. The two additional factors that they found to make a difference in the evaluation of experts beyond simple 'expertise' were trustworthiness and dynamism. Trustworthiness is found in honest and objective witnesses. Trustworthiness may be challenged when it is shown that you have been retained by one side in the case (and perhaps for a substantial fee in the average juror's estimate) and the professional who conducts a court ordered evaluation has an initial advantage here. It may be intimated that you are a 'hired gun' if retained by one side. However, you can control the perception in the area of trustworthiness. The expert is ethically bound not to present a biased case and if data is found that runs counter to the thrust of the retaining lawyer's case he or she is bound to present it. In cross-examination for example, when asked a question that does not assist the side that retained you, do not hesitate to answer in an unbiased manner — 'that's a good question and my response is ...'. This dramatically bolsters the impression that you are indeed trustworthy and have no personal stake in the outcome of the case and that your duty to the court is paramount. It is up to the lawyers to craft the right questions, not you.

The second element of dynamism in an expert's presentation is also key to persuasion. The term is derived from the Greek meaning of 'power'. Most effective teachers know the usefulness of this trait and the expert is essentially a knowledge broker for the courts. The expert should display powerful and energetic speech in a direct and straightforward manner eschewing an abundance of hesitations, qualifiers and overly polite or formal speech. To be dynamic, the expert must be seen as comfortable in the public setting, used to speaking in clear thoughtful sentences, at a measured pace and occasionally using humour and analogies that take complex issues into understandable formats. The expert must increase the volume of their verbalisations and vary the rhythm and pace of answers rather than be monotone to maintain the attention of the courtroom. Technical terms when necessarily used in testimony are quickly translated into meaningful lay equivalents. The expert witness wants to achieve the perception as the trusted country doctor who just happens to have won a Nobel Prize. We have heard of some professionals using anxiolytics prior to appearing in court to achieve a relaxed persona but we do not advocate such use as these agents can dull your cognitive abilities at a time when they have to be at their best. Natural pre-trial anxiety can be converted into the energy needed for a dynamic presentation, and this phenomenon has been cited by many professional actors prior to appearing on stage.

We recommend review of in-depth guides to expert testimony for those professionals who will make court appearances on a regular bases (see Brodsky, 1999, 2004, 2012; Dalby, 2007).

CHAPTER 5

Report Writing in Different Jurisdictions

This chapter provides an overview of some of the key features of the different Western jurisdictions in which psychologists act as expert witnesses. There are many similarities between the legal systems of these countries, all of which are based on English common law. There are, however, also some important differences as the legal system of each country is shaped by its own history and local needs. It is of paramount importance that the psychologist who is acting as an expert witness understands the legal issues that are relevant to the report that he or she has prepared.

United States of America

Description of the Jurisdiction

The United States of America is a federal constitutional republic of fifty states and a federal district (Washington, D.C.). Forty-eight states are contiguous and there are two satellite states, Hawai'i and Alaska. The United States also possesses several territories in the Pacific and the Caribbean. Current population estimates show over 315 million people of a highly diverse ethnic and cultural origin. It is the third largest country by both land area and population; it is the world's largest economy. The United States has the highest incarceration rate and total prison population in the world therefore clearly adopts a widely accepted crime-control model of criminal justice.

The United States of America evolved from thirteen British colonies on the Atlantic seaboard that held strongly individualistic identities and political systems, which were to mould the future development of the country. The original constitution of 1787, which is the supreme legal document, still stands with 27 passed amendments and it defines the relative responsibilities of the federal and state governments.

Like other countries borne of the British colonial system, the United States developed a common law tradition. However, unlike some other offspring, American colonies exerted strong independence not only from Britain but from each other. Each state developed a constitution that is supreme within its borders and all powers not delegated to the federal government are reserved to the states. Each state has its own common law history and has accumulated case law. The Supreme Court of the United States has overriding influence on all law in the country.

The strong constitutional powers of the individual states are often recognised as a 'dual-sovereign' system of law with states as the plenary sovereign and the federal government possessing more limited supreme authority. Criminal law is, therefore, comprised largely of state law and for forensic practitioners this requires specific understanding of the parameters of the state laws and procedures in which they practice as these may differ greatly between states. Normally, the supreme court of a state is the final interpreter of law unless a federal issue is breached or engaged. Such areas of federal focus are evasion of federal income tax, physical attacks on federal officials and interstate criminal actions such as drug trafficking. Like most offspring of common law, all fifty states have independent penal (criminal) codes with labels and definitions of specific criminal acts varying across states. These are readily available on the internet.

Many states recognise the distinctions in the seriousness of crimes categorising them as misdemeanours (literally 'wrong manner or behaviour') or felonies ('evil acts') — borrowed from English tradition. Not all crimes fall in the same categories across states. Judges at the federal level are appointed for life after confirmation from the Senate. In contrast, most state judges are elected. Both systems have several layers of appellate courts superior to trial courts.

Defining the Expert

The evolution of expert evidence in the United States in most observers' viewpoints began with the seminal case *of Frye v. United States* (1923). This was a federal Court of Appeals decision that asserted a technique or procedure has to be established to the point of gaining 'general acceptance' in the field in which it exists before it will be accepted as expert evidence. Under this rule all new procedures, no matter how much a breakthrough in methodology were unlikely to find their way into court until it had accumulated the support of the scientific community.

The next step in expert definition came from the *Federal Rules of Evidence* (702) which provided that 'If scientific, technical, or other specialised knowledge will assist the trier of fact to understand the evidence or to determine a fact in issue, a witness qualified as an expert by knowledge, skill, experience, training or education may testify thereto in the form of an opinion or otherwise'. The information must be 'scientific ... implies a grounding in the methods and procedures of science'. The guidelines developed from this included the following considerations: (a) whether it has been tested using some accepted scientific methodology; (b) whether it has been subject to peer review and publication; (c) whether the known or potential rate of error of the scientific technique justifies its use; and d) whether it has achieved a degree of acceptance within the scientific community. A flexible approach to weighing expert evidence was advocated.

Daubert v. Merrell Dow Pharmaceuticals (1993) was to become the most widely quoted benchmark for expert evidence in the United States. Commonly referred to as simply *Daubert*, its ascendency comes partly as it was authored by the federal Supreme Court justices. It rejected the idea that an expert opinion must have general scientific acceptance but put more emphasis on a helpfulness thrust similar to the *Federal Rules of Evidence.* Again, it accepted a flexible approach with the presiding judge having discretion in the admission of an expert. The Supreme Court in *Daubert* concluded that judges may rely upon the following to evaluate expert evidence: falsifiability, known or potential error rate, peer review or publication and general acceptance. So instead of misinterpreting *Daubert* as replacing *Frye*, it simply said that general acceptance as a stand-alone principle is insufficient. A further case, *Kumho Tire Co. v. Carmichael* (1999) extended the test of reliability to non-scientific evidence with broad discretion granted to the trial judge.

These changes over time in broadening the scope of possible expert evidence did not bring a floodgate of new types of evidence and experts in criminal cases were admitted at the same rates after *Daubert* as before (Groscup, 2004). The *Daubert* decision is federal law and although adopted by many state appellate courts, was muted as to impact and is not universally used across the country. Many types of expert evidence go into a trial without scrutiny under a *Daubert* challenge.

Adjudicative Competencies

Competence to stand trial follows the traditional principles drawn from the British origins of this concept. Forty-seven states allow psychologists to provide direct evidence on this issue. The beginning of modern adjudicative competency in the United States issues from *Dusky v. United States* (1960) in which the Supreme Court held that:

> It is not enough for the district judge to find that 'the defendant is oriented to time and place and has some recollection of events' but that the test must be whether he has sufficient present ability to consult with his lawyer with a reasonable degree of rational understanding – and whether he has a rational as well as factual understanding of the proceedings against him. (p. 789)

Dusky defined the standard of adjudicative competence for federal and many state courts but like many legal writings ambiguity over precise interpretations of wording caused many variations of this guideline. Melton et al.

(2007) argued that competency to stand trial reduces to a two pronged test — the defendant's capacity to understand the criminal process as it applies to him and the defendant's ability to adequately function in that process, primarily through interaction with his or her legal counsel. The impetus for an adjudicative competence evaluation can originate from prosecution or defence sources or the court. A low level of suspicion is all that is necessary to initiate the assessment process and this can be accomplished on an inpatient or outpatient basis. The frequency of such evaluations has been estimated to be between 25,000 and 39,000 per year (Hoge et al., 1997).

Adjudicative competence is a fluid concept focusing on the present and there is not the same debate over addressing the ultimate issue that there is with mental state at offence. This is likely due to higher confidence in the data and that the opinion offered typically has only a temporary effect on the rights of the accused if found incompetent. Judge-clinician agreement on incompetence is very high (Cox & Zapf, 2004) as is inter-clinician agreement on categorical judgements of competence to stand trial even using unstructured interviews (Poythress & Stock, 1980).

Instruments to assist the evaluation of adjudicative competence have been developed by psychologists in the United States and some have been tested with specific populations such as patients with psychotic disorders or mental retardation (Stafford, 2003). Most of these are interview-based instruments that review the competencies suggested by *Dusky*. Sometimes more refined decision making abilities, such as waiving constitutional rights such as the right to counsel, the right to a jury, the right to testify, are overlooked in such evaluations. Like all legal decisions, clinicians are offering opinions only. The completion of a competency to stand trial evaluation (and other related competencies) should include a multi-method approach including interviews, psychological testing and third party information which should include information about the alleged offence.

Trial incompetency is strongly correlated with psychotic disorders but can be influenced by many other factors (substance abuse; mental retardation; sensory impairment). Many patients who are found incompetent to stand trial can be returned to competence and some standards regarding forced return to competence via medication have emerged but not without controversy (see Watters [2005]. A relationship between cognitive deficits and incompetency and norestorability has been found (Schwalbe & Medalia, 2007) leading to treatment recommendations for incompetent individuals. Some states have made provisions to limit the length of confinement for incompetent individuals but some jurisdictions still do not have, in statute, set periods for review of those held because of incompetence to stand trial. Some states have tied maximum confinement to the period that the accused would have received if convicted; others have not. This is for individuals who have not been tried on a criminal offence making the return to competency a high priority for clinicians dealing with this population.

Insanity

It might be argued that despite a large number of legal jurisdictions in the United States, the interpretation and approach to determination of competency to stand trial is relatively uniform. Such is not the case with cases of criminal responsibility or insanity claims across the states. Four states (Kansas, Idaho, Montana, and Utah) have no recognised insanity defence, which leaves legal counsel to argue simple lack of mens rea when a major personal injury crime has been committed by a mentally disturbed individual. Several of these states allow Guilty but Mentally Ill (GBMI) pleas. Twenty-seven states have retained some variation of the McNaughton rules — some requiring both prongs of that defence — while others only require one and some with additional tests. Some like Nevada have bobbled back and forth on the law when the real issue was not the court challenges but what happens after a person is sent to a secure facility. The problem with states that have a Not Guilty by Reason of Insanity (NGRI) law must grapple with the issue of safety when the incarcerated patient becomes well again and, since they are not guilty, must be released. Some jurisdictions such as Michigan have sought the refuge of a GBMI option. Appellate courts in jurisdictions such as Nevada baulked at such change and ruled that defendants are entitled to a full insanity defence in addition to a guilty but mentally ill scenario. The legal argument heard that conditional release of the mentally ill after they have been institutionalised after satisfying an insanity defence is unconstitutional in some states flies in the face of the empirical data on mental disorders which can relapse and a released patient can become a risk again. Under Guilty but Mentally Ill legislation if a hospitalised offender became well again they would be transferred to a regular prison to continue their sentence of incarceration.

All states began with the adopted British approach to insanity rulings but criticisms arose based on specific cases where the rules did not seem to fit the facts but the individual was still considered 'insane'. An alternative, the 'Irresistible Impulse Test' was adopted by the Alabama Supreme Court in 1887. This challenged the largely cognitive element in McNaughton and concluded that even if an accused knew right from wrong, the power to choose between those poles was lost because of mental disease and in fact caused the criminal behaviour. The test began to have some merit (in reading the McNaughton case this was also one of the arguments presented by the defence but never incorporated into the rules) but several states found it unworkable and it survives now only as an adjunct to other insanity legislation (e.g., Colorado, Georgia, New Mexico, Texas, Virginia).

The Durham Rule (product test) was adopted originally by New Hampshire in 1871 (the only state to continue under this test, but later adopted from 1954 to 1972 by the District of Columbia). This argued that the accused is not 'criminally responsible if his unlawful act is the product of a mental disease or defect'. In practice this was hard to implement and was not seen as a viable replacement to McNaughton by other states.

Another more successful variation of insanity legislation occurred in 1962 when the American Law Institute (ALI) defined insanity in a much broader fashion than McNaughton. This test states 'a person is not responsible for criminal conduct if at the time of such conduct as a result of mental disease or defect he lacks substantial capacity either to appreciate the criminality of his conduct or to conform his conduct to the requirements of the law'. By 1982 federal courts and many state courts adopted the ALI test but over time the federal courts and some of the states that had adopted it, returned to the McNaughton approach. Eighteen states now use the ALI definition of insanity. In applying the insanity provisions in the United States, the burden of proof is on the defendant in 35 states (and the District of Columbia) and on the state in 11. In most states, the level of proof when the burden is on the defendant is by a preponderance of the evidence and when the burden rests on the state the level of proof of sanity rises to beyond a reasonable doubt. Federal courts and in Arizona the burden is upon the defendant who must prove insanity by clear and convincing evidence. It seems obvious that the forensic practitioner must be fully aware of the specific legislation in their jurisdiction. The American Psychological Association has assisted in publishing a series of state-specific handbooks for 25 states covering a wide scope of information necessary for psychologists interacting with the law (*Law and Mental Health Professional* series).

An insanity defence in the United States cannot be imposed upon an unwilling accused if an 'intelligent' accused voluntarily wishes to forego the defence. Indeed, some successful insanity defences in the United States have been withdrawn and a retrial resulted in the accused receiving a much longer term in a prison.

Sentencing Principles

Sentencing principles in the United States generally follow meeting one or more of the goals of rehabilitation, incapacitation, deterrence (general and specific) and retribution. The shifts in corrective philosophies have evolved, as in other parts of the world, with the rehabilitation emphasis in the 1970s replaced with more emphasis on a 'tough' approach in the following decades.

As previously noted, the United States ranks first in the westernised societies in the per capita rate of incarceration and length of those terms of imprisonment. A factor that may play into this is the election of judges at the state level. Elected judges one could reasonably assume would reflect the will of their constituents more closely than appointed judges. Since the general public, in repeated surveys, has expressed their expectation that the judiciary 'get tough' on crime, this may have an influence on why the United States stands out from other western countries in incarceration rate. The high level of gun crime in the United States is obviously another factor. Estimates place over two million people in correctional facilities in the United States. The number of adults under community supervision in the United States was 4,814,200 by the end of 2011 (Bureau of Justice Statistics, 2011). An average of $22,650 per year was spent to incarcerate an inmate in a state penitentiary and an average of $22,365 per year for every inmate in federal prison (Department of Justice, Bureau of Justice Statistics, 2004). In comparison, the United States' neighbour, Canada, spent $88,067 per federal inmate in 2006 (four times as much) and $109,699 in 2009 (Corrections and Conditional Release Statistical Overview, 2010).

While judges in the United States are free to consider a wide range of mitigating or aggravating factors in deciding sentences there are narrow ranges of determinate sentences (particularly at the federal level) for some proscribed offence. States are, of course, able to determine the method and range of sentencing for offences in their individualised penal codes. In 1987 federal courts adopted a set of sentencing principles to guide their criminal court decisions. However, since the majority of criminal matters are dealt with at the state level, about half of the states, at the urging of the American Bar Association and American Law Institute, have adopted similar sentencing guidelines. Sentences primarily weight two factors — the behaviour leading to the offence and the defendant's criminal history. A sentencing table assists in determining an intersect between these two variables and obtaining a numerical score. For example, an offender with a longer criminal history will receive a longer sentence for the same offence than an individual without a lengthy criminal history. There are factors that can then move this sentence upward or downward. If the accused committed the offence while suffering from reduced mental capacity and this contributed to the offence, then a downward move of sentence length might occur. However, this excludes self-induced intoxicants and may not apply if the individual is deemed a high risk for violence. There are many arguments against the sentencing table approach to deciding punishment and critics suggest that it may increase rather than decrease sentencing disparity. In plea bargaining, the prosecution may use the sentencing tables to their advantage in suggesting more severe sentences to their defence peers (the vast bulk of criminal offences are disposed of through this process).

It would be fair to say that the character of the state may be reflected in their sentencing practices and there is a high level of variation across states on specific rules and regulations regarding the administration of a sentence. Judges (rather than juries) impose sentences in the vast majority of states. The range of sentences includes incarceration, suspension of all or part of the sentence; may impose conditions on probation including participation in treatment programs and restrictions on relocation. Parole boards exist in most states and operate similarly in considering release into the community after a third of a sentence has been served. Several states have eliminated parole in favor of a determinate sentence that will be served in full. The United States is one of the few western societies to retain capital punishment — a common practice in many countries in centuries past, even for minor offences. In the United States it became restricted to cases of homicide, cases against the state, high-level drug trafficking and crimes against humanity. It is rarely applied even in states retaining the sentencing option. It remains in effect in 29 states and in the federal courts (civilian and military). From 2010 to 2012 the number of persons executed ranged from 43 to 46 per year. Several states with capital penalty options have not implemented them since 1976 (the Supreme Court suspended all executions from 1972 to 1976). Despite the rarity of this ultimate penalty, psychologists have played key roles in addressing competence for execution determinations (Brodsky, Zapf, & Boccaccini, 2001) in ensuring that mentally ill individuals do not receive this judgment.

High-Risk and Habitual Offenders

Most jurisdictions in the United States have repeat offender statues — allowing judges to prescribe heavier penalties for those who persist in offending. The purpose falls within the incapacitation goal of general sentencing philosophies. The identified problem with such legislation is that it mixed violent and non-violent offending with many of the repeat offending (drawing the enhanced sentencing) based on non-violent offences (drugs and property crime) and therefore not justified in line of the incapacitation issue. In such habitual offender cases, psychologists do not play a strong role since rehabilitation will never be tested. In line with this a majority of states have also enacted Mentally Disordered Sex Offender (MDSO) statutes to direct sexual offenders to appropriate treatment programs but with the rise of a more punitive philosophy in corrections some of these have lapsed. Confinement for such programming is often indeterminate resting on the outcome of treatment followed by a risk estimate for release. Debates have escalated over these programs from mental health professionals and legal experts based on issues such as lack of appropriate treatment to the inappropriateness of treating a category called 'sex offenders', which is not a recognised mental health category (see Good & Burnstein, 2010; and Duthie & Saari, 2011 for different views of this issue). Additionally, some states have enacted post-sentence civil confinement of those considered to be 'sexually violent predators' (SVP). Exactly who falls into this category of offender and how that is decided remain critical points. It is obvious however that expert evidence on risk prediction generally and with specific inmates would be relevant in all of these cases. Miller, Kimonis, Otto, Kline, and Wasserman (2012) have recently raised some issues about the reliability of risk assessment measures used in these hearings.

Canada

Canada is the world's second largest country by total area bordered by three oceans and on the south by the contiguous United States. It was formed in 1867 with the union of several British North American colonies. It is a federal state governed by a parliamentary democracy and a constitutional monarch although legislative ties to the United Kingdom no longer exist. Canada is officially bilingual and most federal services are offered in French and English. Current population stands at 35 million and remains among the lowest of countries in population density. It is one of the world's most developed nations ranking ninth in per capita income.

Description of the Jurisdiction

All ten provinces and three territories of Canada follow a common law tradition indicating an affirmation of stare decisis or the principle of adhering to settled points of law by following precedents of past cases. Decisions by the Supreme Court of Canada (SCC) or appellate courts of the same province are definitive in laying boundaries for judges' trial decisions. Decisions by parallel courts at the same level (e.g., decisions by other provincial courts in the same province) and decisions of courts in other provinces are not definitive but are considered persuasive in limiting the range of outcomes of a trial decision given the federal scope of criminal law in Canada (a single national criminal code applies to all provinces and territories). To decide a case outside of these guidelines a judge must show how the case at bar differs from the precedents. There is no prohibition from introducing in argument cases or principles gleaned from other common law countries particularly in complex cases or cases in which there is little history of precedent in Canada.

Since 1892 Canada has had a national criminal code that has been passed by the federal parliament and which is continually modified by case law.

Although the federal government is charged with the responsibility of enacting criminal law, the provinces are responsible for administering it (enforcing and prosecuting crime). Criminal law in Canada is considered an area of public law — crimes are acts against the public good. As a constitutional monarchy these crimes are therefore offences against the monarch and are prosecuted by representatives of the Crown (Crown Attorneys) and charges are officially cited as Regina v. (versus) Accused Person (insert last name). Offences are either indictable or prosecuted by summary conviction. Some criminal acts can be prosecuted by either of these routes, an option of the Crown usually based on perceived seriousness of the act.

The structure of Canadian courts is simple compared to the court system of their southern neighbour. For criminal law, most procedures take place in provincial courts — courts where judges are appointed by elected officials from that province. These are judge only courts. If an accused wishes for a jury trial, they would proceed (after preliminary inquiries at the provincial court) to a trial in the superior courts. Not all offences have this option, however. The superior trial courts have different names such as Court of Queen's Bench in provinces of Alberta, Saskatchewan and Manitoba or the Supreme Court in British Columbia or the Superior Court of Justice in Ontario. The justices in these superior trial courts are appointed by the federal government. The vast majority of criminal matters are dealt with at the provincial level with only more serious matters reserved for the superior trial courts. Superior courts can sit as judge only courts as well as jury courts. Judges in provincial courts are verbally addressed as 'Your Honour' while judges in superior courts continue to be addressed in view of their British origin as 'M'Lord' or 'M'Lady'. Above the two trial courts are two appellate courts — the court of appeal for that province and, if a case proceeds beyond that, to the Supreme Court of Canada that sits in Ottawa in a building adjacent to the parliament buildings.

Defining the Expert

For expert evidence to be admissible in Canada there are legal criteria that must be met. The case defining these parameters was a decision in the matter of *R. v. Mohan* (1994) rendered by the Supreme Court of Canada. Mohan was a paediatrician charged with sexual assault of four-teenaged patients. During his trial, Mohan's defence intended to offer a psychiatrist as an expert on sexual assault. The psychiatrist intended to outline the abnormal characteristics an offender for such crimes must have and that Mohan did not have these (three victims were apparently attacked by a paedophile according to the psychiatrist while the fourth was assaulted by a sexual psychopath). The judge heard the evidence in a voir dire as the Crown felt the evidence was inadmissible. The judge indeed ruled the evidence was inadmissible and a conviction was registered. The conviction at trial was appealed and eventually found its way to the Supreme Court and the decision outlined the scope of expert evidence thereafter. The four criteria required to define an expert were outline by the SCC as:

1. The expert evidence must be relevant. Relevant evidence may still be excluded if:

    a. its probative value is outweighed by its prejudicial effect
    b. the time required to prove its admissibility is not commensurate with its value; or
    c. the trier of fact can be influenced out of proportion to the evidence's reliability and therefore should be excluded where it could be mis-used, distort the fact-finding process or confuse the jury who may be overwhelmed by the 'mystic infallibility' of the evidence.

2. Necessity in assisting the trier of fact. Necessity should not be judged by too strict a standard. To be necessary, the evidence must provide information which likely is not within the experience and knowledge of the trier of fact. Experts must not usurp the function of the trier of fact so that as a result, the trial degenerates into a trial of experts, a danger that can occur with too liberal an approach to admissibility.

3. The evidence must not run afoul of an exclusionary rule.

4. The expert must be one who is shown to have acquired a special skill or knowledge through study or experience in the area for which he or she has been called upon to testify.

Novel science is handled differently than established science under Mohan. The Mohan ruling stated that novel science requires stricter scrutiny obtaining a threshold of reliability. Exactly what that threshold is remains undefined but the call is for legal gatekeepers to look more closely before such expert evidence is accepted. It is rare for a mental health expert's opinion to fall outside the clear boundaries under Mohan and the benchmark for being considered an expert is relatively low.

Fitness to Plead

If an individual is unable to conduct a defence to a criminal charge at any stage of the legal proceedings on account of a mental disorder he or she would be considered unfit. The Canadian adaptation of this early English statute lingered for years without a proper definition — relying upon classic case law. In 1992 the Criminal Code adapted a specific standard developed by a law review commission years prior. All individuals are presumed fit to stand trial unless the court decides (on a balance of probabilities) that the accused is unfit. So the finding of unfitness is a rebuttal of fitness by evidence. Either the defence counsel or Crown representative may raise the issue of fitness. To find unfitness there must be a formal conclusion that the accused has a mental disorder which makes him or her unable to (a) understand the nature or object of the proceedings, (b) understand the possible consequences of the proceedings, or (c) communicate with counsel. The evaluation of fitness to stand trial operates under an assessment order that is generally in force for not more than 30 days but this can be increased to 60 days under extraordinary circumstances. Most of these evaluations (about 90%) take place in an inpatient facility but can be done on an outpatient basis as well. Approximately 5000 fitness evaluations are conducted each year in Canada.

In Canada only medical practitioners have been allowed to conduct court-ordered assessments of key pre-trial legal issues such as fitness or criminal responsibility. This does not mean that a lawyer cannot hire an independent psychologist to challenge elements of these types of evaluations or participate in other non-ordered assessments for court. In reality, most fitness evaluations under court order are conducted by a team which usually involves psychologists and social workers. The material gathered by allied health professionals is submitted to a psychiatrist who incorporates the findings in a report to the court.

Although many of the competency for trial instruments developed in other countries are relevant to Canadian fitness evaluations the Fitness Interview Test Revised (Roesch, Zapf, & Eaves, 2006) was first developed using the fitness criteria in the Canadian Criminal Code and is likely the most widely used formal instrument in this country. The revised edition is now applicable for use in other common law countries as well.

After a finding of unfitness by a judge, all criminal proceedings are halted until fitness can be restored. The judge can order that the defendant be detained in a hospital or for minor crime that the defendant be conditionally discharged and attend regular treatment for their mental health concerns. If the defendant becomes fit, he or she returns to the court proceedings. If he or she remains unfit for more than 90 days, he or she is referred to a review board for assessment and disposition. After that they may be reviewed on an annual basis and the Crown must prove every two years that there remains sufficient evidence to bring the case back to court. If the case is not proved the file is dismissed with the finding of not guilty. The whole process can be 'stop and go' with the fluctuating mental condition of the accused. If it becomes clear that a defendant is very unlikely to ever be restored to fitness because of some permanent impediment then a court can stay proceedings if the accused does not pose a significant threat to the safety of the public.

Insanity

The Canadian courts have had a strong tradition of acceptance of behavioural science and insanity cases are an example of the necessity of such an approach. The seminal case which impacted all common law insanity legislation — McNaughton (see Dalby, 2006) — had a powerful influence of the development of such law in Canada. The McNaughton standards, in place for more than a century in Canada, were reviewed by law reform commissions and government departments and after several decades of debate in 1992 relevant changes in the criminal code were enacted. Among changes the term 'not guilty by reason of insanity' was changed to 'not criminally responsible on account of mental disorder' (NCRMD) and the wording of the section 16 (defining the insanity defence) was rewritten to: 'No person is responsible for an act committed or an omission made while suffering from a mental disorder that rendered the person incapable of appreciating the nature and quality of the act or omission or of knowing that it was wrong'. Review boards — legal bodies mandated to oversee the care and disposition of defendants found unfit and/or not criminally responsible on account of a mental disorder — were created. These boards were required to review each unfit and NCRMD case each year.

NCRMD requires proof beyond a balance of probabilities and the onus is on the party who raises the issue. The defence can of course raise the issue of mental disorder at any time in proceedings and the Crown may raise it after a guilty verdict — arguing that the defendant now requires mental health treatment. In practice this option is rarely taken.

Once a finding of NCRMD is reached by the trier of fact, there are several options for disposition. An absolute discharge (defendant released into the community without restrictions) can be ordered by the court or review board for those who do not pose a threat to the community. A conditional discharge can be imposed (defendant released with certain conditions such as prohibition of alcohol use) and failure to meet the conditions will return some form of incarceration. The court or review board may order the defendant be transferred to a psychiatric inpatient facility. Treatment at such an institution is voluntary unless the mental health condition has deteriorated to a level of incompetency.

Review boards often have psychiatrists and psychologists sit as members in addition to lay citizens and legal experts. In reaching decisions the boards comprehensively review psychological testing, clinical history, risk evaluations, criminal histories and any relevant information in files. Canadian legislation capped the time a defendant can remain in a psychiatric facility under this designation. The period of detainment as NCRMD cannot exceed the amount of time the defendant would have served in prison for the offence committed. If the defendant remains a risk once that time period has expired, he or she may then be committed involuntarily to a secure hospital under provincial legislation.

Dangerous Offenders/Long-Term Offenders

Canada has enacted legislation to deal with repeat offenders though special sentencing provisions. The first of these is Dangerous Offender option which is sought by the Crown for high-risk offenders who commit serious personal injury offences. The Criminal Code (section 753) lays out the following conditions to be weighed:

1) A pattern of behaviour showing a failure to restrain his or her behaviour and likelihood of causing death or injury to other persons, or inflicting severe psychological damage on other persons, through failure in the future to restrain his or her behaviour

2) A pattern of persistent aggressive behaviour by the offender showing a substantial degree of indifference on the part of the offender respecting the reasonably foreseeable consequences to other persons of his or her behaviour

3) Any behaviour by the offender, associated with the offence for which he or she has been convicted, that is of such a brutal nature as to compel the conclusion that the offender's behaviour in the future is unlikely to be inhibited by normal standards of behavioural restraint

4) Has shown a failure to control his or her sexual impulses and a likelihood of causing injury, pain or other evil to other persons through failure in the future to control his or her sexual impulses.

The forensic psychologist will readily see that the likely candidates for these criteria would very probably score highly on instruments such as the PCL-R or other measures of psychopathy. If an offender is found to meet the criteria for sentencing as a Dangerous Offender the courts may impose a sentence of detention in a penitentiary for an indeterminate period.

Another sentencing option is the Long-Term Offender categorisation. Defined in the Criminal Code (section 753), the criteria are as follows:

1) It would be appropriate to impose a sentence of imprisonment of two years or more for the offence for which the offender has been convicted
2) There is a substantial risk that the offender will reoffend and
3) There is a reasonable possibility of eventual control of the risk in the community.

The sentence for this designation, following a trial, is a minimum of two years and supervision in the community for a period not exceeding 10 years. Most individuals who have been designated long-term offenders have a history of sexual offences.

Sentencing Principles

The Canadian Criminal code (Section 718.1) outlines the following:

> The fundamental purpose of sentencing is to contribute, along with crime prevention initiatives, to respect for the law and the maintenance of a just, peaceful and safe society by imposing just sanctions that have one or more of the following objectives:

a) To denounce unlawful conduct;
b) To deter the offender and other persons from committing offences;
c) To separate offenders from society, where necessary;
d) To assist in rehabilitating offenders;
e) To provide reparations for harm done to victims or to the community; and
f) To promote a sense of responsibility in offenders, and acknowledgement of the harm done to victims and to the community.

Judges also consider further principles such as the gravity of the offence and degree of responsibility of offender. Aggravating and mitigating circumstances (such as whether the accused abused a position of trust in relation to the victim) are weighed.

In cases where mental health is a key component, rehabilitation concerns may rise to the top of this collective but even so it must always be viewed in balance with the other functions of sentencing. Presentence psychological reports will review specific diagnostic issues along with treatment needs and often specific local programmes where those needs could be met. Presentence reports constitute the majority of psychological reports prepared in criminal matters in Canada.

Judges in Canada have a great deal of discretion in meting sentences for criminal matters and this is often defined by the 'community' sentiment in the province (different provinces can be graded on a scale of conservativism with regard to sentencing and benchmarks for sentencing are established by the appellate court in that province). There are some mandatory sentencing laws which limit the judge to a minimum or narrow range of sentences regardless of the mitigating circumstances. It is very rare for an offender to receive the maximum sentence under law for any charge less than first-degree murder. The range of sentences includes *absolute and conditional discharges*, which have been cited previously. With discharges the key issue is that the offender is not convicted of an offence and the consequences that flow from a criminal record. *Fines and community service* are the most common options and are typically made in minor criminal cases. Next is *probation*, which is release into the community with general conditions (reporting regularly to their probation officer) and specific conditions pertinent to their needs (refraining from drug use). Failure to meet probation conditions could result in imprisonment for up to two years. *Restitution* is a sentencing option in cases where the victim has suffered financial losses or when a person has been injured to cover medical bills and lost income. The latter purpose is more common as the victim may pursue civil actions for damages and the provinces have criminal injury boards which can grant financial compensation. *Conditional sentence* is an imposed sentence of incarceration, which is allowed to be served in the community. The incarceration is suspended as long as the offender follows the prescribed rules while in the community. The sentence is time limited and failure to abide by the rules may result in incarceration for the term of the sentence. *Imprisonment* tends to be viewed as a sentence reserved when remaining in the community is viewed as inappropriate using the sentencing principles already outlined. Sentences of less than two years are served in provincial jails while sentenced two years or over are served in federal penitentiaries. There are no death penalty provisions in Canada having been abolished in 1976 for offences under the Criminal Code and the last execution occurred in 1962. Several attempts to reinstate such legislation have been unsuccessful. Many Canadians have the perception that the criminal justice system is not harsh enough but this is a general finding across many western societies.

Sentences of incarceration are rarely served to term in Canada. By law, offenders housed in federal penitentiaries must be released with supervision into the community after serving two-thirds of their sentence (statutory release) with offenders serving life sentences not eligible for this release. Statutory release is not a decision of the parole board but offenders who pose a high risk for statutory release may have this privilege blocked. Earlier release through parole options is common and federal offenders are eligible for parole at one third of their sentence of incarceration. Other forms of parole include temporary absences from prison; day parole (offenders take part in community based activities such as work programmes). Full parole allows the offender to serve the remainder of their sentence in the community with reporting to a parole officer required and usually is granted after successful completion of partial parole programmes listed above. Decisions for release on parole are made by the Parole Board of Canada who lean heavily on risk evaluations carried out by psychologists and consider a broad range of information in reaching their conclusions (specifics about current offence; criminal history; mental health and substance use history; performance on earlier releases; information from victims; institutional behaviour; benefits from treatment received etc.).

In Canada the bulk of incarcerations are short (91.2 per cent of women and 85.4 per cent of men are incarcerated for less than six months). Empirical data on the criminal justice system is easily obtained in Canada with the centralisation of this information through Statistics Canada (www.statcan.gc.ca); for example, the number of firearm homicides in the country in 2011 was 158 the lowest rate in almost 50 years (and dramatically lower than our nearest international neighbour — the United States). The incarceration rate in Canada in 2010 was 140.53 per 100, 000 in the general population, making international comparisons easier.

United Kingdom
Description of the Jurisdiction

In the United Kingdom most minor criminal trials take place in magistrates' courts. These courts operate without a jury, and decisions are made either by three unpaid Justices of the Peace (selected from the community) or one legally trained magistrate, using the 'beyond reasonable doubt' criteria. Serious criminal cases are heard in a Crown court in front of a judge and a jury of twelve members of the general public. In 'Fitness to Plead' hearings, however, although decision-making in terms of verdict is made by the jury, and the judge alone is responsible for ensuring a fair trial (as discussed later). Every person over the age of majority is presumed by law to be sane and to be accountable for his or her actions (*R v Layton*, 1849). The onus is thus on the defence to establish insanity at the time of the offence on the balance of probabilities.

Much of the advice that is available to those who seek to appear as an expert witness in United Kingdom courts is consistent with that which is provided throughout this book. The guidelines for expert witness in England, Wales and Northern Ireland published by the British Psychological Society ([BPS], 2010), for example, is an excellent resource for those who are interested in fulfilling this role. The most recent practice directions for expert witnesses can be accessed from the following websites:

https://www.justice.gov.uk/courts/procedure-rules/criminal/docs/2012/crim-proc-rules-2013-part-33.pdf

https://www.justice.gov.uk/courts/procedure-rules/criminal/rulesmenu

The British Psychological Society guidelines underscore the need for experts to assist the Court and not the party(ies) instructing them and to report facts truthfully while also offering an interpretation of those facts where they are relevant to the case and where interpretation would otherwise be beyond the knowledge or experience of the court. Although Scotland has its own legal system and structure of courts, the same general principles apply when experts are invited to give evidence to Scottish courts.

Defining the Expert

Part 33.3 of the Criminal Procedure Rules (2012) requires expert's report to include the following content:

(a) details of the expert's qualifications, relevant experience and accreditation;

(b) details of any literature or other information which the expert has relied on in making the report;

(c) a statement setting out the substance of all facts given to the expert which are material to the opinions expressed in the report, or upon which those opinions are based;

(d) which of the facts stated in the report are within the expert's own knowledge;

(e) who carried out any examination, measurement, test or experiment which the expert has used for the report and

   (i) give the qualifications, relevant experience and accreditation of that person,

   (ii) say whether or not the examination, measurement, test or experiment was carried out under the expert's supervision, and

   (iii) summarise the findings on which the expert relies;

(f) where there is a range of opinion on the matters dealt with in the report

   (i) summarise the range of opinion, and

   (ii) give reasons for his own opinion;

(g) if the expert is not able to give his opinion without qualification, state the qualification;

(h) a summary of the conclusions reached;

(i) a statement that the expert understands his duty to the court, and has complied and will continue to comply with that duty; and

(j) contain the same declaration of truth as a witness statement.

Taylor et al. (2012) have noted that while there may be a single expert in less serious cases, in those which are more serious courts sometimes seek the opportunity to hear from both independent and treating experts. The court may even direct that discussion between experts takes place prior to the trial to identify the common ground and those areas that might be in dispute. The Criminal Procedure Rules (2012) state that where more than one party wants to introduce expert evidence, the court may direct the experts to (a) discuss the expert issues in the proceedings; and (b) prepare a statement for the court of the matters on which they agree and disagree, giving their reasons. However, where more than one defendant wants to introduce expert evidence on an issue at trial, the court may direct that the evidence on that issue is to be given by one expert only. Where the co-defendants cannot agree who should be the expert, the court may — select the expert from a list or identified by them; or direct that the expert be selected in another way. An

Expert Witness directory is published each year that lists eligible witnesses (Pamplin, 2012).

In criminal proceedings, the expert witness generally makes one declaration as follows:

> I am an expert in the field of psychology and I have been requested to provide a statement. I confirm that I have read guidance contained in a booklet known as Disclosure: Experts Evidence and Unused Material — Guidance Booklet for Experts which details my role and documents my responsibilities in relation to my role as an expert witness. I have followed the guidance and recognise the continuing nature of my responsibilities of revelation. In accordance with the duties of revelation, as documented in the guidance booklet I:
> (a) Confirm that I have complied with my duties to record, retain and reveal material in accordance with the Criminal Procedure and Investigations Act 1996, as amended.
> (b) Have compiled an Index of all material. I will ensure that the Index is updated in the event I am provided with or generate additional material.
> (c) That in the event my opinion changes on any material issue, I will inform the investigating officer, as soon as reasonably practicable and give reasons.

The Crown Prosecution Service publication 'Disclosure: Experts' Evidence and Unused Material — Guidance Booklet for Experts' ([CPS], 2010) www.cps.gov.uk/legal/section20/chapter_a_annex_k.html) is another useful source of information for experts who practice in the criminal courts. The publication notes that expert witnesses have three core duties to the court:

> a) 1to *retain* everything until otherwise instructed (retention periods are determined by the investigator);
> b) to *record* everything, starting from instruction (including when you took, received and delivered material and the means, notes and those of assistants which are detailed enough for another expert to follow, own notes of all meetings attended, telephone conversations noting points of agreement, disagreement and agreed actions, and all e-mails); and
> c) to *reveal* everything that has been recorded (in the report, in a formal statement, and through completing an Index of Unused Material).

It is suggested that failing to attend to what are described as these 'core duties' can have a range of serious consequences, for example, leading to unsafe convictions, prosecutions being halted, or an adverse judicial judgement being made against the expert.

Fitness to Plead

The overriding principle as set out in the Practice Direction (Criminal Proceedings: Consolidation) is that a defendant who has a mental disorder within the meaning of the *Mental Health Act 2007*, or some other significant impairment of intelligence and social function that inhibits a full understanding of and participation in the proceedings, should be found unfit.

The Crown Prosecution Service website notes that the mental disorder is designed broadly under Mental Health Act as 'any disorder or disability of the mind'. Examples of clinically recognised mental disorders are provided, including personality disorders, eating disorders, autistic spectrum disorders, mental illnesses such as depression, bipolar disorder and schizophrenia, and learning disabilities. The term 'learning disability', equivalent to the term 'intellectual disability' as used in other parts of the world, refers to 'a state of arrested or incomplete development of the mind which includes significant impairment of intelligence and social functioning' and is a recognised mental disorder. Dependence on alcohol or drugs, however, does not come within the legal meaning of mental disorder unless directly associated with mental disorders. Promiscuity, other immoral conduct, and sexual deviancy are also not recognised as mental disorders.

The procedure for determining fitness to plead is set out in the *Criminal Procedure (Insanity) Act 1964* as amended by the *Criminal Procedure (Insanity and Unfitness to Plead) Act 1991*, although provision is also made in the *Domestic Violence, Crime and Victims Act 2004*. The procedure has two stages:

Stage 1. Whether the offender is under a disability i.e. whether he or she is 'unfit' to plead.

The question of fitness may be raised by the prosecution, defence, or the Judge prior to arraignment. The decision is made by the Judge after receiving written or oral evidence from two or more registered medical practitioners, at least one of whom must be approved under the *Mental Health Act 1983*. It is possible to remand the defendant to hospital for either an assessment (section 35 Mental Health Act) or for treatment (section 36 Mental Health Act), although in the majority of cases it is expected that the defendant will respond to treatment, thus allowing the trial to take place within a reasonable timeframe.

Stage 2. Whether he or she did the act or made the omission charged against him.

If the Judge finds that the defendant is unfit to plead, a jury will then decide whether the defendant did the act or made the omission as charged. The jury should not find that the defendant did the act unless satisfied beyond reasonable doubt that the prosecution has disproved that defence (*R v Antoine* [2000]). If the jury finds that the defendant did the act or made the omission, the court can then remand the defendant to hospital for further assessment or treatment or make an interim hospital order. If the offender becomes fit to plead after a findings of unfitness, then an order for arraignment will be made (*Hasani v Blackfriars Crown Court* [2005]).

It has also been suggested that all possible steps should be taken to assist a vulnerable defendant to understand and participate in the proceedings, even if this means adapting the trial process to achieve this. In *C v Sevenoaks Youth Court* (2009) it was held that the court has an inherent power to appoint an intermediary to assist a defendant to prepare for the trial in advance of the hearing and during the trial so that he or she could participate effectively in the trial process.

In conclusion, this chapter provides a brief overview of some of the key guidance that is available to expert witnesses in the United Kingdom. As in any jurisdiction, it is important that the witness is familiar with this local guidance to ensure that he or she complies with the court requirements and guidance if his or opinion is to be accepted by the court.

Australia

Description of the Jurisdiction

Australia is an island continent surrounded by the Indian, Pacific and Southern Oceans, which was originally settled by the British as a penal colony populated by convicts and military personnel. In 1901, the Australian colonies became a federation through the passing of the Commonwealth of Australia Constitution Act by the British Parliament. Australia today is a federal state governed by a parliamentary democracy and a constitutional monarch, it consists of six states (New South Wales, Victoria, Tasmania, South Australia, Western Australia and Queensland) and two territories (the Northern Territory and the Australian Capital Territory).

The powers of the federal parliament are outlined in the Constitution, with section 51 listing those specific matters on which the Commonwealth has the power to legislate. In the case of conflict, federal law prevails, however federal law can only be passed in relation to matters allowed by the Constitution. The High Court of Australia (established in 1903) determines whether the federal government has such a power where there is a dispute.

The High Court of Australia has a general appellate jurisdiction over the State Supreme Courts, meaning that the High Court acts as a court of appeal for the country as a whole. This ensures there is a single uniform Australian common law. Australian common law is still influenced by United Kingdom Court decisions and also (to a lesser degree), other common law countries such as New Zealand, Canada and the United States.

All states and territories have a supreme court. Supreme Courts are 'superior courts', which means that their decisions are binding on lower courts (unless reversed on appeal). All jurisdictions, apart from Tasmania, the Australian Capital Territory and the Northern Territory, have an intermediate trial court — called a county court in Victoria and district court in the other states. Most jury trials take place in the intermediate trial courts. At the bottom of the court hierarchy are the courts of summary jurisdiction, called Magistrates' Courts or Local Courts (depending on the state jurisdiction). Each state and territory has its own legislation relevant to criminal law, and mental health. It is essential that those conducting psycho-legal assessments are familiar with the legislation of the particular state or territory jurisdiction in which the assessment is conducted.

Mental Impairment

Some jurisdictions have adopted legislation that presumes that defendants are sane, such that insanity is something that has to be proven. In Queensland, for example, every person is presumed to be of sound mind, and to have been of sound mind at any time which comes in question, until the contrary is proved. Similarly in Tasmania, every person is presumed to be of sound mind, and to have been of sound mind at any time which comes in question, until the contrary is proved. The Commonwealth legislation also specifies the presumption of 'sanity', stating that:

> A person is presumed not to have been suffering from such a mental impairment. The presumption is only displaced if it is proved on the balance of probabilities (by the prosecution or the defence) that the person was suffering from such a mental impairment. s7.3(3) *Criminal Code Act 1995*

The terms 'mental illness' or 'mental disorder' have a legal definition that differs between jurisdictions (although there are considerable commonalities). This is important, as any assessment of mental impairment will need to be guided by the specific legislation that is relevant to the jurisdiction in which it is conducted. What is clear is that the language of legislation in any jurisdiction is very complex, very specific, and often very confusing for those outside of the legal professions. Nonetheless, conviction and often imprisonment for an individual may rely on the appropriate interpretation of the relevant legislation by the assessing professional. It is therefore extremely important that psychologists and other professionals generally unfamiliar with legal language become familiar and comfortable with the terminology, and more importantly the intended meaning of such terms.

The extent to which someone may have a mental impairment may constitute grounds for a legal defence against a criminal charge. The term 'mental impairment' has a legal meaning in Australian states and territories, although definitions vary between jurisdictions depending largely on the period in which the legislation was written and the terminology of the time. For example, in Tasmania reference is made to 'natural imbecility' — a term rarely used in contemporary mental health or legal contexts. The term 'imbecility' was originally coined to describe individuals whose intellectual functioning was in a specific range.

The defence of 'mental impairment' (or what is sometimes referred to in the common vernacular as the 'insanity' defence) generally serves to legally excuse an accused offender from criminal responsibility for their conduct because of an inability to know the nature and quality of the conduct or to know that the conduct was wrong. Such a conception is based on the traditional common law M'Naghten Rules, the most well known of which states:

> [T]o establish a defence on the ground of insanity, it must be clearly proved that, at the time of the committing of the act, the party accused was laboring under such defect of reason, from disease of the mind, as not to know the nature and quality of the act he {or she} was doing; or, if he {or she} did know it, that he {or she} did not know he {or she} was doing what was wrong.

While there have been some calls to develop uniform legislation across all Australian jurisdictions, it is clear that the states and territories all depart from the model defence as set out in the *Criminal Code Act 1995* (Cth), which defines impairment as 'senility, intellectual disability, mental illness, brain damage, or severe personality disorder', such that the offender did not know the nature and quality of the conduct, did not know that it was wrong, and/or was unable to control the conduct. All legislation refers to the nature, quality and wrongfulness of the conduct, the main distinction lies in the inclusion or exclusion of a volitional component.

Fitness to Stand Trial

There is a general principle in law that a person must be deemed 'fit' to be able to both plead and stand trial. Usually, if a person charged with an offence is found unfit for trial and the unfitness for trial is of a permanent nature, then proceedings against the person for the offence are discontinued and further proceedings are not taken against them.

The states and territories also differ in the specific details of legislation concerning an individual's fitness to plead or to stand trial. Again, as with the legislation concerning mental incompetence or impairment at the time of committing an offence, legislative differences across Australian jurisdictions concerning those who are deemed unfit to proceed to trial vary more in their precise terminology than in the substantive concepts which they embrace. There are more similarities than differences. In general terms, definitions of fitness in Australian jurisdictions cover most (if not all) of the following considerations:

- understanding of the nature of the charge
- capacity to enter a plea to the charge
- ability to understand the nature of the proceedings
- ability to follow proceedings and/or understand the evidence presented against them

- capacity to exercise procedural rights
- capacity to make a defence
- ability to instruct a lawyer to act on their behalf.

Preventative Detention

Specialist legislation has been introduced within Australian states and territories to address cases in which there is a view that the risk of the defendant re-offending is so high that the sentence applied should be indefinite. The terms used to apply to these situations are preventative detention or indeterminate sentencing. Legislation has been drafted in relation to cases of both violent and sexual offending.

New Zealand

Description of the Jurisdiction

New Zealand (Aotearoa in the indigenous Māori language) is a small island country in the southwestern Pacific Ocean, with a total population of approximately four and half million people. The capital of New Zealand, Wellington, is situated in the North Island, with the South Island constituting the other main land mass.

In 1840, the Treaty of Waitangi was signed between the British Crown and the Māori, the indigenous people of New Zealand. It established British law in New Zealand and is considered New Zealand's founding document and an important part of the country's history. New Zealand is a constitutional monarchy with a parliamentary democracy; it has the advantage over some of the other commonwealth jurisdictions discussed in this book by having a single national jurisdiction.

The highest court in New Zealand is the Supreme Court, with most criminal matters being heard in the District Court. Within the District Court's jurisdiction are offences ranging from very serious offending such as rape, aggravated robbery, and sexual violation down to minor offences such as disorderly behaviour. The only charges that cannot be heard by the District Court are murder, manslaughter and Class A drug offences, and a small number of other very serious crimes. The New Zealand justice system also includes a number of specialist courts and tribunals outside of the courts of general jurisdiction, including the Waitangi Tribunal, the Māori Land Court, the Family Court, Youth Court and Environment Court.

Guiding Legislation

The *Crimes Act 1961* forms a leading part of the criminal law in New Zealand, and sets out the specific nature of a range of crimes against the person, against public order, affecting the administration of law and justice, as well as crimes against religion, morality, public welfare and personal privacy. The Act outlines the maximum penalties for selected offences and also 'matters of justification or excuse', including the defence of 'Insanity'.

A major piece of legislative reform and development was undertaken in 2003 with the introduction of the *Criminal Procedure (Mentally Impaired Persons) Act 2003*. The Act enshrined the need for special options and processes for mentally impaired people coming before the Court on criminal charges, providing the first significant revision of this area of the law in New Zealand since 1954. When considering the 'mentally impaired population', the Act made a clear distinction between people with a mental illness and those with intellectual disability, thereby addressing a gap in the law which had resulted in a lack of provision for the particular needs of people with an intellectual disability.

In 2004, the New Zealand Parliament introduced the Parole (Extended Supervision) Amendment Act that permits the correctional supervision (in the community) of child sex offenders for up to 10 years after the completion of their finite sentence. An extended supervision order (ESO) is intended to enhance the safety of the community from individuals who 'pose a real and ongoing risk of committing sexual offences against children or young persons' (section 107I(1) as cited in Ryan, Wilson, Kilgour, & Reynolds, 2014), and their implementation has generated considerable interest and debate amongst psychologists in New Zealand. In particular, concerns have been raised regarding the predictive validity of static risk measures used in the determination of who should be considered for an ESO, and the objectivity of correctional psychologists tasked to carry out the assessments (see Vess, 2009). Recent research suggests that a higher number of dynamic risk factors are most predictive of an ESO being recommended (Ryan et al., 2014).

Mental Impairment

Consistent with the M'Naghten rules adopted in most commonwealth jurisdictions and outlined previously, the *Crimes Act 1961*, Part 3, section 23 states:

> No person shall be convicted of an offence by reason of an act done or omitted by him when labouring under natural imbecility or disease of the mind to such an extent as to render him incapable —
> (a) Of understanding the nature and quality of the act or omission; or
> (b) Of knowing that the act or omission was morally wrong, having regard to the commonly accepted standards of right and wrong.

In December 2010 the Law Commission of New Zealand published an extensive report entitled *Mental Impairment Decision-Making and the Insanity*

Defence, which examined the various difficult issues associated with section 23 (not least of all the outdated terminology) and rather interestingly concluded that 'there are occasions in the law where significant change cannot be undertaken because a demonstrably better set of rules cannot be designed. This is one of those occasions' (p. iv). This report contains a rigorous discussion of the complex issues associated with the administration and application of the law in New Zealand, and should be consulted further by anyone considering (or currently engaging in) practice in this area.

Fitness to Plead

Section 4 of the *Criminal Procedure (Mentally Impaired Persons) Act 2003* (the Interpretation section) sets out the grounds by which a person can be deemed unfit to participate in the court process:

> unfit to stand trial, in relation to a defendant, —
> (a) means a defendant who is unable, due to mental impairment, to conduct a defence or to instruct counsel to do so; and
> (b) includes a defendant who, due to mental impairment, is unable—
> (i) to plead:
> (ii) to adequately understand the nature or purpose or possible consequences of the proceedings:
> (iii) to communicate adequately with counsel for the purposes of conducting a defence.'

The introduction of the Act in 2003 meant that the threshold definition for unfitness to stand trial (which had previously been called 'under disability') was 'mental impairment' rather than 'mental disorder' (thus extending the provision to those with intellectual disability). Other significant changes included the requirement for the Court to make a determination that the defendant 'caused the act or omission in question' before a finding of unfitness could be made, and introduced new rights of appeal against a finding of fitness.

The Act also aligned maximum periods of detention with current parole eligibility rules (with the maximum increasing from 7 to 10 years for those found unfit as a 'special patient' (if mentally disordered) or as a 'special care recipient' (if intellectually disabled). Interestingly, decisions about a change in status (either that a person's condition has improved to the extent that they are no longer unfit, or that they no longer require detention) rest with the Attorney-General and/or the Minister of Health. This is the case both for those found unfit, and those deemed 'criminally insane', and as such would seem vulnerable to the same concerns raised in United States' jurisdictions about the possible partiality of elected officials making decisions about detention or release in high profile cases. Not surprisingly therefore, recent reviews have recommended that this be changed (New Zealand Law Commission, 2010).

Sentencing

As in other commonwealth jurisdictions, the goals of sentencing in New Zealand are retribution and denunciation; deterrence (both specific and general); incapacitation; rehabilitation; and restitution. Regardless of the intended goals, the main guiding principles of sentencing, are usually considered to be:

- restraint/minimum intervention;
- equality before the law (freedom from discrimination);
- equality of impact; and
- controlling public expenditure (Ministry of Justice, 1997).

The ethical dilemma's inherent in balancing these often incompatible principles are not unique to this jurisdiction, and are most prominent in consideration of offenders classified as 'dangerous', and whom are deemed to be of greatest risk to the community.

In New Zealand there is no provision in law to hold a person perceived as dangerous in prison after their finite sentence has expired. The opportunity to impose an indefinite period of protective confinement occurs at the sentencing stage, through the imposition of preventive detention (an indefinite sentence, with a standard non-parole period of 10 years). Amendments to the Criminal Justice Act in 1993 allow sentencing judges to impose a non-parole period longer than ten years in 'exceptional cases', with no limit on the non-parole period which the judge may impose (Ministry of Justice, 1997).

While these provisions are aimed at serious violent offenders, there have been concerns raised that Māori people may be particularly disadvantaged by the classifications and methods used to arrive at a determination that an individual is so dangerous that they should be detained for what they might do in future

Local Guidance for Expert Witnesses

In New Zealand, there are two tests to determine the admissibility of expert evidence: (a) 'utility' — that the issue being considered is far beyond a jury's understanding thereby requiring the expert's evidence; and (b) 'risk' — that the evidence is sufficiently reliable and 'vetted', such that the jury can accept it without undue risk (Henderson & Seymour, 2013). The definition of an expert witness is set out in the *Evidence Act 2006* and the specific obligations and expectations of experts giving evidence in the courts in New Zealand is provided by the Code of Conduct for Expert Witnesses (Schedule 4 of the *Judicature Act 1908*). The code states:

Schedule 4

Code of conduct for expert witnesses

Schedule 2 Schedule 4: replaced, on 1 February 2009, by section 8(1) of the Judicature (High Court Rules) Amendment Act 2008 (2008 No 90).

Duty to the court

1. An expert witness has an overriding duty to assist the court impartially on relevant matters within the expert's area of expertise.
2. An expert witness is not an advocate for the party who engages the witness.

Evidence of expert witness

3. In any evidence given by an expert witness, the expert witness must—

    (a) acknowledge that the expert witness has read this code of conduct and agrees to comply with it:

    (b) state the expert witness' qualifications as an expert:

    (c) state the issues the evidence of the expert witness addresses and that the evidence is within the expert's area of expertise:

    (d state the facts and assumptions on which the opinions of the expert witness are based:

    (e) state the reasons for the opinions given by the expert witness:

    (f) specify any literature or other material used or relied on in support of the opinions expressed by the expert witness:

    (g) describe any examinations, tests, or other investigations on which the expert witness has relied and identify, and give details of the qualifications of, any person who carried them out.

4. If an expert witness believes that his or her evidence or any part of it may be incomplete or inaccurate without some qualification, that qualification must be stated in his or her evidence.
5. If an expert witness believes that his or her opinion is not a concluded opinion because of insufficient research or data or for any other reason, this must be stated in his or her evidence.

Duty to confer

6. An expert witness must comply with any direction of the court to —

    (a) confer with another expert witness:

    (b) try to reach agreement with the other expert witness on matters within the field of expertise of the expert witnesses:

    (c prepare and sign a joint witness statement stating the matters on which the expert witnesses agree and the matters on which they do not agree, including the reasons for their disagreement.

7. In conferring with another expert witness, the expert witness must exercise independent and professional judgment, and must not act on the instructions or directions of any person to withhold or avoid agreement.

Schedule 2 Schedule 4 clause 7: replaced, on 1 December 2009, by rule 10 of the High Court Amendment Rules (No 2) 2009 (SR 2009/334).

As in other jurisdictions, the New Zealand Psychological Society (NZPS) sets out further requirements for psychologists in the *Code of Ethics for Psychologists Working in Aotearoa/New Zealand* with respect to areas of practice and a necessary cognisance of the limitations of one's experience and knowledge.

Consideration of issues pertaining to the examination of expert witnesses in the New Zealand criminal and family law courts has been comprehensively reviewed and qualitatively researched in a recent publication conducted on behalf of the Law Foundation of New Zealand by Henderson and Seymour (2013). They found that expert witnesses are reluctant to involve themselves in the court process, and concluded that there was substantial room for improvement in terms of 'the court process and the support structures around the expert witness' (p. 145). Local research looking at New Zealand jurors (Blackwell, 2007) found that they tended to prefer experiential expertise over the purely academic (93% of jurors in the study preferred experts with professional experience, while only 47% saw high academic qualifications as increasing an expert's credibility). Being easy to understand and appearing to be even-handed were also considered to make an expert more believable.

One specific area of practice in which psychologists can provide expert evidence in New Zealand is in 'Mode of Evidence' applications, whereby psychologists can assist the court by providing an opinion about the necessity or otherwise of a witness or complainant giving their evidence in extraordinary ways (such as via CCTV, privacy screens or pre-recorded interview). The NZPS provides further specific guidance for psychologists providing such a service to the court, by way of the practice resource *Psychologists as Expert Witnesses: Guidelines Concerning Modes of Evidence Applications* (2010), available on the NZPS website. This document provides a number of recommendations relevant to providing expert psychological evidence in general, and is consistent with the information and suggestions provided throughout this book.

Singapore

Description of the Jurisdiction

Singapore is a small but densely populated country with a resident population of just over five million people. It is near the equator, located south of

Malaysia, South-East Asia, and although made up of over 60 different islands, has a total land mass of only 272 square miles (704 km^2). Singapore is a relatively new country that only became independent in 1965 when it separated from the Federation of Malaysia after a long period of British rule. Mr Lee Kuan Yew, Singapore's senior minister and Prime Minister for more than 40 years following independence, developed a strong vision of how Singapore should be governed that has profoundly shaped not only the economic development of the country but also the current criminal justice system. In the words of the then Chief Justice, Chan Sek Keong (2006): 'Singapore has a worldwide reputation for being tough on crime and tough on the causes of crime' (p. 1). According to Hor (2000), the major thrust of government policy was, for many years, 'the progressive removal of 'obstacles' to conviction, severe punishment of the convicted; and where conviction is not possible, executive detention as a fallback' (p. 1). For example, since 1959 detention without trial has been used in relation to suspected terrorists, criminals, gangs, secret societies and, insurgents (Criminal Law [Temporary Provisions] Act), and unlawful possession of any arm or ammunition is considered a serious offence that is punishable by imprisonment for not less than five years and not more than ten years. The anti-drug trafficking laws are among the toughest in the world, including provision for drug addicts to be detained without trial for the purpose of rehabilitation (see Chan Sek Keong, 2006). Jury trials were abolished in 1969 and the Criminal Procedure Code was amended in 1992 to allow for trials of capital offences to be heard before a single judge. These laws are supported by tough punishments, including the death penalty and caning, both mandatory and discretionary.

At the same time the Singapore prison system has, over the last decade, embraced the notion of evidence-based practice in correctional service delivery. Guided by the research evidence that rehabilitation works beyond just incarcerating offenders (e.g., Andrews & Bonta, 2010), the Singapore government has made a deliberate and concerted effort to develop offender rehabilitation initiatives in correctional settings. Chua Chin Kiat, an ex-director of the Singapore Prison Service paved the way for change resulting in the creation of the Prison Vision (see Day & Casey, 2012):

> We aspire to be Captains in the lives of offenders committed to our custody. We will be instrumental in steering them towards being responsible citizens, with the help of their families and the community. We will thus build a secure and exemplary prison system.

Neo (2010) has identified six discrete strategies that have helped the Singapore Prison Service achieve these goals. The first strategy, the employment of established risk/needs tools, saw the introduction of a case management system that determined rehabilitation pathways based on assessed risk of re-offence and criminogenic need. The second involved the development of a suite of offending behaviour programs and a commitment to program evaluation. The next steps were to develop a throughcare and reintegration framework, to mobilise the community, and to set up a network of community providers and agencies to support prisoners following their release. The final strategy has been to develop the capabilities of correctional workers. These strategies offer those jurisdictions that have yet to fully embrace rehabilitative ideals the basis of a template for service development or for reflection on their current status.

Guiding Legislation

The Singaporean criminal justice system has a strong British colonial legacy, and Singapore courts interpret the legal codes in much the same way as occurs in any system of common law. However, the origins of the modern legal system in Singapore can be traced back to the Straits Settlements of 1867. Chan Sek Keong (2006) suggests that the three basic laws of criminal justice are Indian in origin. For example, the Penal Code, enacted in 1870, was based substantially on the Indian Penal Code of 1860. The first Criminal Procedure Code, enacted in 1870, was based on the Indian Act XVIII of 1862, and the current Code was enacted in 1900 based on the Indian Code. Finally, the Evidence Act, enacted in 1893, was also based on the Indian Act of 1872. In recent years, however, many of the provisions in the Criminal Procedure Code and the Evidence Act have been modified to encourage the repression of criminal conduct or what has been referred to as the 'crime control' model (Packer, 1984). For example, in 1976 the Criminal Procedure Code was amended to incorporate the recommendations of the 11th Report of the United Kingdom Criminal Law Committee by modifying the right to silence. Suspects, when arrested, are not allowed to have immediate access to counsel. A suspect still has a right not to answer a question that may incriminate him, but any omission by the police to inform him of this right will not affect the admissibility of any admission he makes. Chan Sek Keong illustrates this by referring to the rules regarding an accused person's testimony as follows:

> Upon his arrest, an accused did not have to answer any incriminating questions. His silence during interrogation could not be raised as a relevant consideration at trial. In addition, even when the accused provided statements to the police, the rules of evidence treated these statements as being generally inadmissible. This rule extended to an accused's confessions, unless they had been made in the presence of a magistrate. During the trial itself, an accused could continue to maintain his silence with impunity. Where he so desired, he could even elect to give unsworn evidence in lieu of evidence on oath.

The principal source and starting point for the law of evidence in Singapore is nonetheless the Evidence Act 1997 (Revised Edition). The Law Reform

Committee (2011) describes the Evidence Act as a comprehensive code that repeals all inconsistent rules of evidence at common law. The committee notes, however, that 'simply reading the Evidence Act with modern eyes and without an appreciation of its history is a recipe for confusion, at least until the entire Act is overhauled, rationalised and modernised' (Coomaraswamy & Singapore Academy of Law, 2011).

In Singapore, mentally ill offenders who are arrested by the police can be referred to mental health services for voluntary treatment, detained under the Mental Health (Care and Treatment) Act 2008, or formally charged. Those who have been charged with crimes that attract mandatory capital punishment (such as murder and some forms of drug trafficking) are remanded at Changi Prison Hospital for security reasons. The court has powers, under Chapter 68 of the Criminal Procedure Code, to remand an accused person to a psychiatric hospital for observation for up to one month if the Judge is not satisfied that the accused is capable of making his defence. The pre-trial psychiatric examination examines the person for the presence of mental illness, fitness to plead (competency to stand trial), whether the person was criminally responsible and makes recommendations to the court regarding treatment. Following trial, those found incompetent or unfit to stand trial can be committed to hospital under the Criminal Procedure Code, or under a different section if acquitted on the grounds of insanity (see Yap, Sim, & Lim, 1999).

There is a general principle in law that a person must be deemed fit to be able to both plead and to stand trial. Usually, if a person charged with an offence is found unfit for trial and the unfitness for trial is of a permanent nature, then proceedings against the person for the offence are discontinued and further proceedings are not taken against them. Under the present law of Singapore the courts do not have any discretion to proceed with the trial once the issue of fitness to plead has been raised (see section 307(1) of the Criminal Procedure Code).

A person is deemed competent to stand trial if he is able to understand the charge, the possible consequences, and the difference between a plea of guilty and not guilty, to instruct counsel, and to follow evidence in court. A person is deemed criminally responsible (to be of sound mind) if s/he knew the nature or quality of the act and knew that what he or she did was wrong (see Yap, Sim & Lim, 1999). Cheang (1998) provides a critique of the fitness to plead provisions in Singapore, noting that the Code does not define the phrase 'unsoundness of mind', or set out the factors that may be relevant for the court to take into account in determining whether an accused is incapable of making his or her defence. Cheang sees the term 'unsoundness of mind' is broadly equivalent to the English law use of the terms 'insanity' and notes that that 'unsoundness of mind' by itself will not amount to unfitness; it must be a type that renders the accused incapable of conducting his own defence. In the absence of local guidance on establishing fitness, Cheang suggests that reference is made to English principles. These concern the need for the accused to have a general comprehension of the proceedings and the evidence. In practice, any investigation into an accused's fitness to stand trial draws on medical expertise. In Singapore such an investigation may be held in the absence of the accused if the court is satisfied that, owing to the accused's mental condition, 'it would be in the interests of the safety of the accused or of other persons or in the interests of public decency that he should be absent' (Cheung, 1999).

Local Guidance for Expert Witnesses

The General Acceptance Test is used to determine the role of expert witnesses in the court process. An expert witness is thus someone who is recognised by the court as a person who can give an opinion in a specific area of knowledge that the court determines is outside the understanding of the common man. In other words expert testimony will not be admissible unless the subject matter of the trial involves issues beyond the competence of a lay jury [or court] to determine if unaided by such experts. However, in Singapore, the courts have generally adopted a strict approach to the common knowledge rule. Consider the Court of Appeal case of *Chou Kooi Pang & Anor v PP*:

> The first appellant was charged with drug trafficking. He called an expert to support his defence that he was a person of borderline intelligence and an innocent courier. The defence expert stated that the first appellant had an IQ of 79 and was predisposed to be 'simple minded, naive of people's motives, and shallow in critical thinking'. Yong Pung How CJ held that the trial judge was right to reject the expert evidence. He cited Turner, stating that it is well-established that expert opinion is admissible only to furnish the court with scientific information which is likely to be outside the experience and knowledge of a judge. The Chief Justice also cited Masih where the court expressed the view that in the case of an IQ which, though low, was within the range of normality as understood by psychologists, the admission of expert evidence was not justified. Yong CJ concluded that on the facts, the question whether the first appellant suspected he was carrying drugs was a matter entirely within the trial judge's purview. Reiterating one of the main justifications for the common knowledge rule, he stated: 'A chief and justified concern of the courts is that the fact-finding process should not be surrendered to professionals such as psychiatrists, but should remain the province of the courts.

It appears then that the courts in Singapore do not subscribe to the more flexible approach to the common knowledge rule that has been adopted in countries like Australia and New Zealand. Expert evidence in these cases is received only when it is necessary for the judge to understand abnormality.

The Singapore courts have adopted a flexible approach to who qualifies as an expert. In *Leong Wing Kong v PP Yong Pung*, How CJ said: 'The competency of an expert is a question for the court. Considerable laxity prevails with regard to the issue of who an expert is'. In *PP v Muhamed bin Sulaiman* it was observed that: '… while an expert must be 'skilled', he need not be so by special study, he may be so by experience, and the fact that he has not acquired his knowledge professionally goes merely to the weight and not admissibility' (see Coomaraswamy, & Singapore Academy of Law, 2011).

The Law Reform Committee on Opinion Evidence has recently released a series of recommendations relevant to expert testimony. The report noted that admission of expert evidence is regulated by section 47 of the Evidence Act, which provides as follows:

> Opinions of experts
>
> 47. — (1) When the court has to form an opinion upon a point of foreign law or of science or art, or as to the identity or genuineness of handwriting or finger impressions, the opinions upon that point of persons specially skilled in such foreign law, science or art, or in questions as to the identity or genuineness of handwriting or finger impressions, are relevant facts.
>
> (2) Such persons are called experts.

The committee recommended that the Act be amended to read as follows:

> Opinions of experts
>
> 47. — (1) When the court has to form is likely to derive substantial assistance from an opinion upon a point of scientific, technical or other specialized knowledge, such an the opinion is a relevant fact.
>
> (2) Such persons with such specialised knowledge or skill based on training, study or experience are called experts.
>
> (3) The opinions of an expert may be relevant facts even if the opinions relate to a matter of common knowledge.
>
> (Coomaraswamy & Singapore Academy of Law, 2011)

The proposed amendments make the test of 'assistance' and not 'necessity' the overarching basis of admissibility of expert evidence, but require that the assistance that the court expects to derive must be 'substantial'. Further, the court must consider it 'likely' that the opinion will render the requisite level of assistance. Specified, enumerated fields of expertise are replaced with the general phrase 'scientific, technical or other specialised knowledge'. This is intended to broaden the types of evidence that may be admitted, which provides more scope for expert psychological evidence to be presented. In conclusion then, it appears that while there is currently only a limited scope for psychologists in Singapore to provide expert testimony more opportunities may arise in the future. It is incumbent on those who work in this jurisdiction to be familiar with the guiding legislation and provide high quality forensic assessments such that psychological opinion becomes more widely recognised as providing substantial assistance to judicial decision-making.

References

Andrews, D.A., & Bonta, J. (2010). Rehabilitating criminal justice policy and practice. *Psychology, Public Policy, and Law, 16,* 39–55.

Anthony, T. (2010). *Sentencing indigenous offenders, Brief 7, Indigenous Justice Clearinghouse.* State of New South Wales through the Department of Justice and Attorney General.

Bank, S.C., & Poythress, N.G. (1982). The elements of persuasion in expert testimony. *The Journal of Psychiatry & Law, 10,* 173 –204.

Ben-Porath, Y.S., & Tellegen, A. (2011). *MMPI-2-RF (Minnesota Multiphasic Personality Inventory-2 Restructured Form): Manual for administration, scoring, and interpretation.* Minneapolis, MN: University of Minnesota Press.

Benson, E. (2003). Rehabilitate or punish? *Monitor on Psychology, 34,* 46–47.

Blackwell, S. (2007). *Child sexual abuse on trial* (Unpublished doctoral thesis). University of Auckland.

Boccaccini, M.T., Murrie, D.C., & Duncan, S.A. (2006) Screening for malingering in a criminal-forensic sample with the Personality Assessment Inventory. *Psychological Assessment, 18,* 415–423.

Briere, J. (1995). *Trauma Symptom Inventory: Professional manual.* Odessa, FL: Psychological Assessment Resources.

British Psychological Society. (2010). *Psychologists as expert witnesses: Guidelines and procedure for England, Wales and Northern Ireland* (3rd ed.). Leicester, England: British Psychological Society.

Brodsky, S.L. (1999). *The expert expert witness: More maxims and guidelines for testifying in court.* Washington, DC: American Psychological Association.

Brodsky, S.L. (2004). *Coping with cross-examination and other pathways to effective testimony.* Washington, DC: American Psychological Association.

Brodsky, S.L. (2012). *Testifying in court: Guidelines and maxims for the expert witness* (2nd ed.). Washington, DC: American Psychological Association.

Brodsky, S.L., Zapf, P.A., & Boccaccini, M.T. (2001). The last competency: An examination of legal, ethical and professional ambiguities regarding evaluations of competence for execution. *Journal of Forensic Psychology Practice, 1*, 1–25.

Casey, S., Day, A., Ward, T., & Vess, J. (2012). *Foundations of offender rehabilitation*. Oxford, England: Routledge.

Chan Sek Keong (2006). *From Justice model to Crime Control model*. Presentation at the International Conference on Criminal Justice under Stress: Transnational Perspectives. November 24, 2006, New Delhi, India.

Chartrand, L.N., & Forbes-Chilibeck, E.M. (2003). The sentencing of offenders with Fetal Alcohol Syndrome. *Health Law Journal, 11*, 35–70.

Cheung, M. (1988). Fitness to plead in Singapore and Malaysia. *Anglo-American Law Review, 209*.

Cohen, F. (2008). *The mentally disordered inmate and the law* (2nd ed.). Kingston, NJ: Civic Research Institute.

Coomaraswamy, V., & Singapore Academy of Law (2011). *Report of the Law Reform Committee on Opinion Evidence*. Singapore Academy of Law.

Corrections and Conditional Release Statistical Overview (2010). Retrieved from www.publicsafety.gc.ca/res/cor/rep/2010

Cox, M.L., & Zapf, P. (2004). An investigation of discrepancies between mental health professionals and the courts in decisions about competency. *Law and Psychology Review, 28*, 108–131.

Criminal CodeCrown Prosecution Service. (2010). *Disclosure: Experts' evidence and unused material – guidance booklet for experts*. Retrieved from www.cps.gov.uk/legal/section20/chapter_a_annex_k.html

Dalby, J.T., & Nesca, M. (2008) Forensic psychology and document reviews. *American Journal of Forensic Psychology, 26*, 5–16.

Dalby, J.T. (2006). The case of Daniel McNaughton: Let's get the story straight. *American Journal of Forensic Psychiatry, 27*, 17–32.

Dalby, J.T. (2007). On the witness stand: Learning the courtroom tango. Canadian *Family Physician, 53*, 65–70.

Day, A., & Casey, S. (2012). Transformational change in correctional services: Offender rehabilitation and reintegration in Singapore. In *Trends in corrections: Interviews with corrections leaders around the world*. London, England: CRC Press, Taylor and Francis Group in conjunction with IPES.

Day, A., Nakata, M., & Howells, K. (Eds.) (2008). *Anger and Indigenous men*. Annandale, NSW: Federation Press.

Douglas, K.S., Hart, S.D., Webster, C.D., Belfrage, H., & Eaves, D. (2008). *HCR: Assessing Risk for Violence (Version 3, Draft 1.0)*. Burnaby, BC, Canada: Mental Health, Law, and Policy Institute, Simon Fraser University.

Duellman, R.M., & Bowers T.G. (2004). Use of the Personality Assessment Inventory (PAI) in forensic and correctional settings: Evidence for concurrent validity. *International Journal of Forensic Psychology, 1*, 42–57.

Duthie, B., & Saari, R. (2011). Response to 'A modern day witch hunt: The troubling role of psychologists in sexual predator laws'. *American Journal of Forensic Psychology, 29*, 49–59.

Edens J.F., Cruise K.R., & Buffington-Vollum, J.K. (2001). Forensic and correctional applications of the Personality Assessment Inventory. *Behavioral Sciences and the Law, 19*, 519–543.

Edens, J.F., Hart, S.D., Johnson, D.W., Johnson, J.K., & Olver, M.E. (2000). Use of the Personality Assessment Inventory to assess psychopathy in forensic populations. *Psychological Assessment, 12*, 132–139.

Finland Ministry of Justice. (2009). The Criminal Code of Finland [trans]. Author. Retrieved from http://www.finlex.fi/en/laki/kaannokset/1889/en18890039

Gacono, C.B., Evans, F.B., & Viglione, D.J. (2002). The Rorschach in forensic practice. *Journal of Forensic Psychology Practice, 2*, 33 –53.

Good, P., & Burstein, J. (2010). A modern day witch hunt: The troubling role of psychologists in sexual predator laws. *American Journal of Forensic Psychology, 28*, 23–49.

Greenberg, S.A., & Shuman, D.W. (1997). Irreconcilable conflict between therapeutic and forensic roles. *Professional Psychology: Research and Practice, 28*, 50–57.

Groth-Marnatt, G. (2009). *Handbook of psychological assessment* (5th ed.). Chichester, England: Wiley.

Grisso, T. (2010). Guidance for improving forensic reports: A review of common errors. *Open Access Journal of Forensic Psychology, 2*, 102–115.

Groscup, J.L. (2004). Judicial decision making about expert testimony in the aftermath of Daubert and Kumho. *Journal of Forensic Psychology Practice, 4*, 57–66.

Haney, C. (1980). Psychology and legal change: On the limits of a factual jurisprudence. *Law and Human Behavior, 17*, 371 –398.

Hathaway, S.R., & McKinley, J.C. (1940). *The Minnesota Multiphasic Personality Inventory manual.* New York, NY: Psychological Corporation.

Helmes, E. (1993). A modern instrument for evaluating psychopathology: The Personality Assessment Inventory Professional Manual. *Journal of Personality Assessment, 61*, 414–417.

Helmus, L., Hanson, R.K., & Thornton, D. (2009). Reporting Static-99 in light of new research on recidivism norms. *The Forum, 21*, 38–45.

Henderson, E., & Seymour, F. (2013). *Expert witnesses under examination in the New Zealand Criminal and Family Courts.* Law Foundation of New Zealand.

Hoge, S.K., Bonnie, R.L., Poythress, N., Monahan, J., Eisenberg, M., & Feurcht-Havier, T. (1997). The MacArthur Adjudicative Competence Study: Development and validation of a research instrument. *Law and Human Behavior, 21,* 141–179.

Hor, M. (2000). Sing*apore's innovations to due process.* Paper presented at the International Society for the Reform of Criminal Law at the Conference on Human Rights and the Administration of Criminal Justice, Johannesburg, South Africa.

Kessler, R.C., Barker, P.R., Colpe, L.J., Epstein, J.F., Gfroerer, J.C., Hiripi, E. ... Zaslavsky, A.M. (2003). Screening for serious mental illness in the general population. Archives of General Psychiatry, 60, 184–189.

Kucharski, L.T., Petitt, A.N., Toomey, J., & Duncan, S. (2008). The utility of the Personality Assessment Inventory in the assessment of psychopathology. *Journal of Forensic Psychology Practice, 8,* 344–357.

Lezak, M.D., Howieson, D.B., Bigler, E.D., & Tranel, D. (2012). *Neuropsychological assessment* (5th ed.). Oxford, England: Oxford University Press.

McCann, J.T. (2002). Guidelines for forensic application of the MCMI-III. *Journal of Forensic Psychology Practice, 2,* 55 –69.

Meloy, R. (1992). *Violent attachments.* Northvale, NJ: Jason Aronson.

Melton, G.B., Petrila, J., Poythress, N.G., & Slobogin, C. (2007). Psychological evaluations for the courts: A handbook for mental health professionals and lawyers (3rd ed.). New York, NY: Guilford Press.

Messing, J.T., & Thaller, J. (2013). The average predictive validity of intimate partner violence risk. *Journal of Interpersonal Violence, 28,* 1537–1558.

Miller, C.S., Kimonis, E.R., Otto, R.K., Kline, S.M., & Wasserman, A.L. (2012). Reliability of risk assessment measures used in sexually violent predator proceedings. *Psychological Assessment, 24,* 944–953.

Morey L.C. (2007). *Personality Assessment Inventory manual.* Lutz, FL: Psychological Assessment Resources.

Nesca, M., & Dalby, J.T. (2013). *Forensic interviewing in criminal court matters.* Springfield, IL: C.C. Thomas.

Neo, L.H. (2009). *Offender rehabilitation and reintegration — a Singaporean model.* Paper presented at the ACEA – Reintegration Puzzle Conference.

New Zealand Law Commission. (2010). *Mental impairment decision-making, and the insanity defence. Law Commission Report, 120.* Author.

New Zealand Ministry of Justice. (1997). *Sentencing policy and guidance: A discussion paper.* Author.

New Zealand Ministry of Justice. (2003*). Guide to the Criminal Procedure (Mentally Impaired Persons) Act 2003.* Author.

Otto, R.K. (2002). Use of the MMPI-2 in forensic settings. *Journal of Forensic Psychology Practice, 2,* 71–91.

Pamplin, C. (2012). *UK Register of expert witnesses: Expert witness year book 2012.* Newmarket, England: J.S. Publications.

Pope, K., Butcher, J.N., & Seelen, J. (1993). The MMPI, MMPI-2 & MMPI-A in court. Washington, DC: American Psychological Association.

Poythress, N.G., & Stock, H. (1980). Competency to stand trial: A historical review and some new data. *Journal of Psychiatry and the Law, 8,* 131–140.

Roesch, R., Zapf, P.A., & Eaves, D., (2006). *The Fitness Interview Test — Revised (FIT-R).* Sarasota, FL: Professional Resources Press.

Rogers, R., Bagby, R.M., & Dickens, S.E. (1992). *Structured Interview of Reported Symptoms (SIRS) Professional manual.* Odessa, FL: Psychological Assessment Resources.

Rogers, R., & Ewing, C.P. (2003). A prohibition of ultimate opinions: a misguided enterprise. *Journal of Forensic Psychology Practice, 3,* 65–75.

Ryan, J., Wilson, N., Kilgour, G., & Reynolds, N. (2014). Balancing efficiency and accuracy: Guidelines for the psychological assessment of extended supervision orders for child sex offenders in New Zealand. *Psychiatry, Psychology and Law, 21,* 139–157.

Savage C.R., Baer L., Keuthen N.J., Brown H.D., Rauch S.L., & Jenike M.A. (1999). Organisational strategies mediate non-verbal memory in Obsessive Compulsive Disorder. *Biological Psychiatry, V45,* 905–916.

Schwalbe, E., & Medalia, A. (2007). Cognitive dysfunction and competence restoration: Using cognitive remediation to help restore the unrestorable. *Journal of the American Academy of Psychiatry and Law, 35,* 518 –525.

Seymour, F., Blackwell, S., & Thorburn, J. (2010). *Psychology and the law in Aotearoa New Zealand.* Wellington: New Zealand Psychological Society.

Stafford, K.P. (2003). Assessment of competence to stand trial. In A.M. Goldstein & I.B. Weiner (Eds.), *Handbook of psychology: Volume 11, Forensic Psychology.* New York, NY: John Wiley & Sons.

Strauss, E., Sherman, E.M. S., & Spreen, O. (2006). *A compendium of neuropsychological tests: Administration, norms and commentary* (3rd ed.). New York, NY: Oxford University Press.

Streissguth, A.P., Bookstein, F.L., Barr, H.M., Sampslon, P.D., O'Malley, K., & Young, J.K. (2004). Risk factors for adverse life outcomes in fetal alcohol syndrome and fetal alcohol effects. *Developmental and Behavioral Pediatrics, 25,* 228 –238.

Taylor, P.J., Graf, M., Schanda, H., & Vollm, B. (2012). The treating psychiatrist as expert in the courts: Is it necessary or possible to separate the roles of physician and expert? *Criminal Behavior and Mental Health, 22,* 271–292.

Tillbrook, C., Mumley, D., & Grisso, T. (2003). Avoiding expert opinions on the ultimate legal questions: The case for integrity. *Journal of Forensic Psychology Practice, 3,* 77–87.

Vess, J. (2009) Fear and loathing in public policy: Ethical issues in laws for sex offenders. *Aggression and Violent Behavior, 14*, 264–272.

Watters, T. (2005). Competence to stand trial with forced medication: Placing defendants in harm's way? *Journal of Forensic Psychology Practice, 5*, 79 – 88.

White L.J. (1996) Review of the Personality Assessment Inventory (PAI): A new psychological test for clinical and forensic assessment. *Australian Psychologist, 31*, 38–39.

Yap, H.L., Sim, L.P., & Lim, C.C. (1999). Psychiatric survey of offenders under criminal commitment in Singapore. *Singapore Medical Journal, 40*, 2–8.

Appendix

Example Practice Direction

The Supreme Court of South Australia, Practice Direction 46A outlines what is expected if a person is to be accepted by the court as an expert. This Practice Direction is reproduced below as an example of the requirements for recognition as an expert in the Supreme Court of South Australia, Australia.

SUPREME COURT OF SOUTH AUSTRALIA Practice Direction No. 46A

Guidelines for Expert Witnesses in Proceedings in the Supreme Court of South Australia — Dated 17th May 2002

1. These guidelines apply to all actions in which the pleadings have closed on or after 3 June 2000.
2. These guidelines are not intended to address exhaustively all aspects of an expert's report and an expert's duties.
3. These guidelines, however, must be complied with for an expert to comply with r 38.01A(2)(d).
4. General duty to the Court:

    4.1 An expert witness has an overriding duty to assist the Court on matters relevant to the expert's area of expertise.

    4.2 An expert witness is not an advocate for a party.

    4.3 An expert witness's paramount duty is to the Court and not to the person retaining the expert.

5. The form of the expert report:

    5.1 An expert's written report will set out with reasonable particularity all of the qualifications of the expert which are relied upon to qualify the expert to give the report.

    5.2 It will set out separately all of the factual findings or assumptions upon which any opinion is based.

5.3 The report will give particulars identifying the material upon which the expert bases his or her expert opinion.

5.4 If any tests or experiments are relied upon by the expert in compiling the report, the report should contain details of the qualifications of the person who carried out any such tests or experiments.

5.5 Where an expert's report refers to photographs, plans, calculations, analyses, measurements, survey reports or other extrinsic matter, these must be provided to the opposite party at the same time as the delivery of the report.

5.6 The report should set out separately from the factual findings or assumptions each of the opinions which the expert expresses.

5.7 The expert should give reasons for each opinion.

5.8 If an expert opinion is not fully researched because the expert considers that insufficient data is available — or for any other reason, this must be stated with an indication that the opinion is no more than a provisional one. Where an expert witness who has prepared a report believes that it may be incomplete or inaccurate without some qualification, that qualification must be stated in the report.

5.9 The expert should make it clear when a particular question or issue falls outside his or her field of expertise.

5.10 The expert's report will contain an acknowledgement at the commencement of the expert's report that the expert has been provided with this practice direction prior to preparing the expert's report and that the expert has read it and understood it.

5.11 At the end of the report the expert should declare that (the expert) has made all the inquiries which "(the expert) believes are desirable and appropriate and that no matters of significance which (the expert) regards as relevant have, to (the expert's) knowledge, been withheld from the Court."

6. The further obligations of an expert and the party retaining the expert:

6.1 If, after exchange of reports or at any other stage, an expert witness changes his or her view on a material matter, having read another expert's report or for any other reason, the change of view should be communicated in writing (through legal representatives) without delay to each party to whom the expert witness's report has been provided and, when appropriate, to the Court.

6.2 The party who has retained the expert will, if requested by a party to whom an expert's report has been delivered, deliver to that party:

6.2.1 A list of all documents which have been referred to, or prepared by or at the direction of the expert in the course of preparing the report.

6.2.2 Copies of any documents in the list delivered pursuant to 6.2.1.

6.2.3 Details of any fee, disbursement or benefit received, or receivable, by the expert or anyone on his or her behalf, for the preparation of the report and for services provided, or to be provided, by the expert or by any one on his or her behalf in connection with the expert giving evidence for the party in the action;

6.2.4 A list of all conversations in which the expert has taken part with any party, any legal representative of a party or any other expert consulted in relation to the matter relevant to the opinions expressed in the report stating when and with whom each such conversation occurred and the topics discussed;

6.2.5 Copies of all notes made by or on behalf of the party or by or on behalf of the expert concerning any of the conversations referred to in a list provided under the previous obligation.

7. The expert's evidence:

An expert's evidence in chief at the trial unless the Trial Judge otherwise allows is to be given only by tendering the reports from the expert which comply with r 38 and the expert swearing that the reports are correct.

8. Consequences of non disclosure:

If a party fails to comply with the Rules of Court or this Practice Direction in respect of an expert's report:

8.1 The Court may adjourn the hearing or trial at the cost of the party in default or his or her solicitor.

8.2 The Court may direct that evidence from that expert not be adduced by that party at the trial in the action.

8.3 The Trial Judge may award costs to the other parties or reduce costs otherwise to be awarded to the party in default.

8.4 The Trial Judge may take that failure, if it be by a plaintiff, into account in assessing the award of damages to the plaintiff.

9. Expert's conference:

9.1 If experts retained by the parties meet at the direction of the Court, or at the request of solicitors for the parties it would be improper conduct for an expert to be given or to accept instructions not to reach agreement. If, at a meeting directed by the Court, the experts cannot reach agreement on matters of expert opinion, they should specify their reasons for being unable to do so.

10. Experts employed by a party to the action:

The provisions and requirements of r 38 and this Practice Direction apply to any person called as an expert in the action, even if the expert is employed by a party to the action.

Glossary of Psychological Test

Categorising Psychological Tests
Performance Tests
Intelligence Tests
Full Version
Stanford-Binet Intelligence Scales, 5th Edition (SB5)
Wechsler Adult Intelligence Scale, 4th Edition (WAIS–IV)
Wechsler Intelligence Scale for Children, 4th Edition (WISC-IV)
Short Version
Kaufman Brief Intelligence Test, 2nd Edition (KBIT-2)
Test of Nonverbal Intelligence, 4th Edition (TONI-4)
Universal Nonverbal Intelligence Test (UNIT)
Wechsler Abbreviated Scale of Intelligence, 2nd Edition (WASI-II)
Wechsler Abbreviated Scale of Intelligence (WASI)

Achievement Tests
Wide Range Achievement Test 4
Kaufman Functional Academic Skills Test (K-FAST)
Basic Achievement Skills Inventory (BASI)

Literacy
Progressive Achievement Tests in Reading (PAT-R)
Compass Literacy Assessment

Numeracy
Advanced Numerical Reasoning Appraisal
Compass Numeracy Assessment

Developmental Tests
Autism Spectrum
Asperger Syndrome Diagnostic Scale (ASDS)
Asperger's Syndrome Test

Autism Diagnostic Interview, Revised (ADI-R)
Autism Test
Childhood Autism Rating Scale, Second Edition (CARS2)
Gilliam Asperger's Disorder Scale (GADS)
Gilliam Autism Rating Scale, 2nd Edition (GARS-2)
PDD Behavior Inventory (PDDBI™)
PDD Behavior Inventory Screening Version (PDDBI-SV)
PDD Behavior Inventory Screening Version for PARiConnect (PDDBI-SV)
Social Communication Questionnaire (SCQ)
Social Responsiveness Scale (SRS)
The Australian Scale for Asperger's Syndrome
The Pervasive Developmental Disorder

Attention Deficit/Hyperactivity Disorder Test (ADHD)
ADHD Symptoms Rating Scale (ADHD-SRS)
Behavior Rating Inventory of Executive Function–Adult Version (BRIEF-A)
Brief Test of Attention (BTA)
Children's Color Trails Test (CCTT)
Clinical Assessment of Attention Deficit–Adult and Clinical Assessment of Attention Deficit–Child (CAT-A CAT-C)
College ADHD Response Evaluation (CARE)
Color Trails Test (CTT)
Comprehensive Trail-Making Test (CTMT)
Digit Vigilance Test (DVT)
NAB Digits Forward/Digits Backward Test
NAB Numbers & Letters Test
Tasks of Executive Control™ (TEC)
Test of Variables of Attention, Version 8 (T.O.V.A.8)

Adaptive Behavior Tests
Adaptive Behavior Assessment System Second Edition (ABAS 2)
Vineland Adaptive Behavior Scales, Second Edition (Vineland-II)

Self-Report Tests/Checklists

Personality
NEO Personality Inventory-Revised (NEO PI-R)
OMNI Personality Inventory and OMNI-IV Personality Disorder Inventory (OMNI OMNI-IV)
Structured Interview for the Five-Factor Model of Personality (SIFFM)
The NEO Inventories: NEO Personality Inventory-3 (NEO-PI-3)
OMNI Personality Inventory (OMNI)
16 Personality Factors Questionnaire (16PF – Fifth Edition)
Nonverbal Personality Questionnaire (NPQ)

Eysenck Personality Questionnaire - Revised (EPQ-R)
Minnesota Multiphasic Personality Inventory-2-RF (MMPI-2-RF)
Millon Clinical Multiaxial Inventory-III (MCMI-III)

Psychopathology
Personality Assessment Inventory (PAI)
Adolescent Psychopathology Scale (APS)
Symptom Checklist-90-Revised (SCL-90-R)
Personal Problems Checklist
Hare Psychopathy Checklist Screening Version (PCL:SV)
Hare Psychopathy Checklist-Revised: (PCL-R) 2nd Edition
Structured Clinical Interview for DSM-IV Axis 1 (SCID-I) and Axis 2 (SCID-II)

Specific Clinical
Health
General Health Questionnaire (GHQ)

Stress
Life Stressors and Social Resources Inventory (LISRES-A and LISRES-Y) (LISRES)
Depression, Anxiety & Stress Scale (DASS)

Anxiety
Multidimensional Anxiety Questionnaire (MAQ)
State-Trait Anxiety Inventory (STAI)
Visual Analog Mood Scales (VAMS)
Beck Anxiety Inventory (BAI)

Depression
Beck Depression Inventory–II (BDI–II)
Clinical Assessment of Depression (CAD)
Reynolds Depression Screening Inventory (RDSI)
Visual Analog Mood Scales

Self-Esteem/Self-Concept
Beck Hopelessness Scale (BHS)
Cognitive Distortion Scales (CDS)
College Adjustment Scales (CAS)
Culture Free Self-Esteem Inventories, 3rd Edition (CFSEI-3)
Inventory of Altered Self-Capacities (IASC)

Multidimensional Self-Esteem Inventory (MSEI)
Tennessee Self-Concept Scale, 2nd Edition (TSCS:2)

Pain
Psychosocial Pain Inventory (PSPI)
Behavioral Assessment of Pain Questionnaire (BAP -2)

Trauma
Trauma Symptom Inventory (TSI)
Detailed Assessment of Post Traumatic Stress (DAPS)
Posttraumatic Stress Diagnostic Scale (PDS)
PTSD Checklist Civilian Version

Bhavioural

Eating Disorder
Eating Disorder Inventory (EDI-3)
Eating Inventory

Addictions — Gambling
G-MAP Maroondah Assessment Profile for Problem Gambling

Addictions — Substance Use
Adolescent Drinking Index (ADI)
Adolescent SASSI-A2 (SASSI-A2)
Alcohol Use Inventory (AUI)
Substance Abuse Subtle Screening Inventory - Third Edition (SASSI-3)

Interest (e.g., Vocational)
Career Attitudes and Strategies Inventory (CASI)
Career Decision Scale (CDS)
Career Thoughts Inventory (CTI)
Employee Assistance Program Inventory (EAPI)
Occupational Stress Inventory-Revised (OSI-R)
Self-Directed Search 5th Edition Form R (SDS)

Combination Performance/Self-Report/Checklists
Risk and Needs Assessment
Offending Behaviour
Inventory of Offender Risk, Needs, and Strengths (IORNS)
Reynolds Adolescent Adjustment Screening Inventory (RAASI)
PAI Interpretive Report for Correctional Settings for PARiConnect
Psychosocial Evaluation & Threat Risk Assessment (PETRA)

Level of Service/Case management Inventory (LS/CMI)
Dynamic Risk Assessment for Offender Re-entry (DRAOR)

Suicidal Behaviour
Beck Suicide Inventory
Firestone Assessment of Self-Destructive Thoughts
Firestone Assessment of Suicide Intent (FAST™-FASI)
Suicidal Ideation Questionnaire (SIQ)
Beck Scale for Suicide Ideation (BSS)

Sex Offending
Sexual Violence Risk-20 (SVR-20)
Multiphasic Sex Inventory
STABLE-2007
Juvenile Sexual Offending Assessment Protocol (JSOAP-II)

Spousal Violence
Spousal Assault Risk Assessment (SARA – second edition)
Ontario Domestic Assault Risk Assessment (ODARA)

Violent Offending/Aggressive Behavior
Adolescent Anger Rating Scale (AARS)
State-Trait Anger Expression Inventory–2 (STAXI-2)
Classification of Violence Risk (COVR)
Firestone Assessment of Violent Thoughts (FAVT)
HCR-20: Assessing Risk for Violence (Version 3) (HCR-20)
Structured Assessment of Violence Risk in Youth (SAVRY)
Violence Risk Scale (VRS)
Violence Risk Appraisal Guide (VRAG)

Response Bias (e.g. Malingering)
Test of Memory Malingering (TOMM)
Inventory of Legal Knowledge (ILK)
Miller Forensic Assessment of Symptoms Test (M-FAST)
Structured Interview of Reported Symptoms, 2nd Edition (SIRS-2)
Structured Inventory of Malingered Symptomatology (SIMS)
Victoria Symptom Validity Test (VSVT)

Psycho-Legal (Fitness or Competency, Criminal Responsibility)
Evaluation of Competency to Stand Trial–Revised (ECST-R)
Rogers Criminal Responsibility Assessment Scales (R-CRAS)
Fitness Interview Test (FIT)

The Evaluation of Competency to Stand Trial-Revised (ECST-R)
MacArthur Competence Assessment Tool for Fitness to Plead (MacCAT-FP)

Corrections Specific Tests
Street Survival Skills Questionnaire (SSSQ)
Carson Personality Assessment

Index

Achievement (tests of), 24,157
Addiction, 28,46,48,160
Adjudicative competency, 113
Alcohol, 10,14-15,28,40,44,46-48,74-75,82,88,130,160
    Fetal alcohol, 51,54,55,59
Anxiety, 26-27,43-43,48,66,69-70,94,159

Behaviour (during assessment), 17,23,42, 64

Care provision, 3
Case formulation, 15
Cognitive functioning, 13,23,42,59,65
Competency, 23,34,47,113-115,122-123,144,161-162
Confidential (ity); limits of, 4-6,8-9,17
Court (appearing in), 108
Court guidelines (see Practice Direction), 4, 6-7,127,129,153
Criminal history, 14,64,117,126
Criminal procedure rules, 128
Criminal responsibility, 35,115,122,133,161
Cross-examination, 97,99,104-108

Daubert, 113
Depression,
Diagnosis (see also DSM and ICD), 22-23,26,31,46,36,99,159
DSM-5, 22,46,69,79
Dual roles/relationships, 4
Durham Rule, 116
Dusky, 113-114

Evidence, 2,9,19,34,97-99,101-106,112-113,116,120-122,128-130,137-144
Examination in chief, 99,103
Expert witness, 6,92,127,132

Federal Rules of Evidence,122
Fetal alcohol (see Alcohol)
File review, 4
Fitness to stand trial (see competency)

Frye, 112-113

Gambling, 14,28,38,41,45-48,64,160

ICD-10, 22
Impression bias (see impression management)
Impression management, 20,32,108
Insanity (see criminal responsibility)
Intellectual functioning (see cognitive functioning)
Kumho Tire Co., 113

Malingering, 32, 33-34,53,105
McNaughton rules, 35,115-116,123
Mens rea, 115
Mohan, 120-121
Neuropsychological assessment, 23-24,46,68

Not criminally responsible (see not guilty by reason of insanity)
Not guilty by reason of insanity, 115,123

Oath, 100-101,104,106,141
Offender rehabilitation, 36,48,129
Oral evidence, 6,97,119

Personality Assessment Inventory (PAI), 25-26,33,43,53,56,66
Pain, 27,46,48,61,124,160
Personal history, 9,11,37160
Personality tests, 25
Physical health, 12,39,55,63,68
Post-trial consultation, 107
Practice direction (awareness of), 4, 6-7,127,129,153
Projective tests, 25
Proof (-ing; getting qualified), 100-102
Psychological tests (validity; reliability, copyright), 18-24
Psychopathy, 31,77,124,159

Qualifications, 2,4,7-8,99,101-102,128,138,153-154

Re-direct, 107
Referral details, 6
Response bias (see impression management)

Review boards, 123
Risk assessment, 29-31,77,92,119,161

Self-esteem, 28,57,159-160
Stress, 12-13,22,26-27,32,58,66,159-160
Structure (of reports), 5
Structured assessments, 17,158-159
Subpoena, 98-100
Substance use, 13,26,28,30,40,58,67,69,78,80,160
Suicide, 26,31-32,44-45,161

Trauma, 9,13,27,32-33,51,53,65-69,76-77,160
Treating practitioner, 2

Ultimate issue, 104,114
Vocational tests, 28

Voir dire, 101,120

Wechsler intelligence scales, 19,23,55,157
Witness of fact, 2

www.ingramcontent.com/pod-product-compliance
Lightning Source LLC
Chambersburg PA
CBHW050140240426
43673CB00043B/1744